MW00845837

Set Up Your Own IPsec VPN, OpenVPN and WireGuard Server

ISBN 979-8987508909

Table of Contents

1 Introduction

1.1 Why build your own VPN

In today's digital age, online privacy and security have become increasingly important. Hackers and other malicious actors are constantly looking for ways to steal personal information and sensitive data, making it essential to take necessary measures to safeguard our online activities.

One way to enhance online privacy and security is by building your own virtual private network (VPN), which can offer a range of benefits:

1. Increased privacy: By building your own VPN, you can ensure that your internet traffic is encrypted and hidden from prying eyes, such as your internet service provider. Using a VPN can be especially useful while utilizing unsecured Wi-Fi networks, such as those found in coffee shops, airports, or hotel rooms. It can help protect your online activities and personal data from being tracked, monitored, or intercepted.

2. Greater security: Public VPN services can be vulnerable to hacks and data breaches, which can expose your personal information to cybercriminals. By building your own VPN, you can have greater control over the security of your connection and the data that is transmitted over it.

3. Cost-effective: While there are many public VPN services available, most of them require a subscription fee. By building your own VPN, you can avoid these costs and have more control over your VPN usage.

4. Access to geographically-restricted content: Some websites and online services may be restricted in certain regions, but by connecting to a VPN server located in another region, you may be able to access content that is otherwise unavailable to you.

5. Flexibility and customization: Building your own VPN allows you to customize your VPN experience according to your specific needs. You can choose the level of encryption you want to use, the location of the server, and the network protocol such as TCP or UDP. This flexibility can help you optimize your VPN for specific activities such as gaming, streaming, or downloading, providing a seamless and secure experience.

Overall, building your own VPN can be an effective way to enhance online privacy and security while also providing flexibility and cost-effectiveness. With the right resources and guidance, it can be a valuable investment in your online security.

1.2 About this book

This book is a comprehensive guide to setting up your own IPsec VPN, OpenVPN and WireGuard server. Chapters 2 through 10 cover IPsec VPN installation, client setup and management, advanced usage, troubleshooting and more. Chapters 11 and 12 cover IPsec VPN on Docker and advanced usage. Chapters 13 through 15 cover OpenVPN installation, client setup and management. Chapters 16 through 18 cover WireGuard VPN installation, client setup and management.

IPsec VPN, OpenVPN and WireGuard are popular and widely used VPN protocols. Internet Protocol Security (IPsec) is a secure network protocol suite. OpenVPN is an open-source, robust and highly flexible VPN protocol. WireGuard is a fast and modern VPN designed with the goals of ease of use and high performance.

1.3 Getting started

1.3.1 Create a cloud server

As a first step, you will need a cloud server or virtual private server (VPS) to create your own VPN. For your reference, here are some popular server providers:

- DigitalOcean (https://www.digitalocean.com)

- Vultr (https://www.vultr.com)
- Linode (https://www.linode.com)
- OVH (https://www.ovhcloud.com/en/vps/)
- Hetzner (https://www.hetzner.com)
- Amazon EC2 (https://aws.amazon.com/ec2/)
- Google Cloud (https://cloud.google.com)
- Microsoft Azure (https://azure.microsoft.com)

First, choose a server provider. Then refer to the tutorial links or example steps for DigitalOcean below to get started. When creating your server, it is recommended to select the latest Ubuntu Linux LTS or Debian Linux (Ubuntu 22.04 or Debian 12 at the time of writing) as the operating system, with 1 GB or more memory (RAM).

- How to set up a server on DigitalOcean
  https://www.digitalocean.com/community/tutorials/how-to-set-up-an-ubuntu-20-04-server-on-a-digitalocean-droplet
- How to create a server on Vultr
  https://serverpilot.io/docs/how-to-create-a-server-on-vultr/
- Getting started on the Linode platform
  https://www.linode.com/docs/guides/getting-started/
- Getting started with an OVH VPS
  https://docs.ovh.com/us/en/vps/getting-started-vps/
- Create a server on Hetzner
  https://docs.hetzner.com/cloud/servers/getting-started/creating-a-server/
- Get started with Amazon EC2 Linux instances
  https://docs.aws.amazon.com/AWSEC2/latest/UserGuide/index.html
- Create a Linux VM in Google Compute Engine
  https://cloud.google.com/compute/docs/create-linux-vm-instance
- Create a Linux VM in the Azure portal
  https://learn.microsoft.com/en-us/azure/virtual-machines/linux/quick-create-portal

Example steps to create a server on DigitalOcean:

1. Sign up for a DigitalOcean account: Go to the DigitalOcean website (https://www.digitalocean.com) and sign up for an account if you haven't already.

2. Once you're logged in to the DigitalOcean dashboard, click the "Create" button in the top right corner of the screen and select "Droplets" from the dropdown menu.

3. Select a datacenter region based on your requirements, e.g. closest to your location.

4. Under "Choose an image", select the latest Ubuntu Linux LTS version (e.g. Ubuntu 22.04) from the list of available images.

5. Choose a plan for your server. You can select from various options based on your needs. For a personal VPN, a basic shared CPU plan with regular SSD disk and 1 GB memory is likely sufficient.

6. Select "Password" as the authentication method, then enter a strong and secure root password. For your server's security, it is crucial that you choose a strong and secure root password. Alternatively, you may use SSH keys for authentication.

7. Select any additional options such as backups and IPv6 if you want.

8. Enter a hostname for your server and click "Create Droplet".

9. Wait a few minutes for the server to be created.

Once your server is ready, you can connect to the server using the username `root` and the password you entered when creating the server.

1.3.2 Connect to the server

Once your server is created, you can access it via SSH. You can use the terminal on your local computer or a tool like Git for Windows to connect to your server using its IP address and your login credentials.

To connect to your server using SSH from Windows, macOS or Linux, follow the steps below:

1. Open the terminal on your computer. On Windows, you can use a terminal emulator like Git for Windows.

Git for Windows: https://git-scm.com/downloads
Download the portable version, then double-click to install. When finished, open the `PortableGit` folder and double-click to run `git-bash.exe`.

2. Type the following command, replacing `username` with your username (e.g. `root`) and `server-ip` with your server's IP address or hostname:

```
ssh username@server-ip
```

3. If this is your first time connecting to the server, you may be prompted to accept the server's SSH key fingerprint. Type "yes" and press enter to continue.

4. If you are using a password to log in, you will be prompted to enter your password. Type your password and press enter.

5. Once you are authenticated, you will be logged in to the server via SSH. You can now run commands on the server through the terminal.

6. To disconnect from the server when finished, simply type the `exit` command and press enter.

You are now ready to create your own VPN!

2 Set Up Your Own IPsec VPN Server Using Auto Setup Scripts

View this project on the web: https://github.com/hwdsl2/setup-ipsec-vpn

Set up your own IPsec VPN server in just a few minutes, with IPsec/L2TP, Cisco IPsec and IKEv2.

An IPsec VPN encrypts your network traffic, so that nobody between you and the VPN server can eavesdrop on your data as it travels via the Internet. This is especially useful when using unsecured networks, e.g. at coffee shops, airports or hotel rooms.

We will use Libreswan (https://libreswan.org) as the IPsec server, and xl2tpd (https://github.com/xelerance/xl2tpd) as the L2TP provider.

2.1 Features

- Fully automated IPsec VPN server setup, no user input needed
- Supports IKEv2 with strong and fast ciphers (e.g. AES-GCM)
- Generates VPN profiles to auto-configure iOS, macOS and Android devices
- Supports Windows, macOS, iOS, Android, Chrome OS and Linux as VPN clients
- Includes helper scripts to manage VPN users and certificates

2.2 Quick start

First, prepare your Linux server* with an install of Ubuntu, Debian or CentOS. Then use this one-liner to set up an IPsec VPN server:

```
wget https://get.vpnsetup.net -O vpn.sh && sudo sh vpn.sh
```

* A cloud server, virtual private server (VPS) or dedicated server.

Your VPN login details will be randomly generated, and displayed when finished.

Optional: Install WireGuard and/or OpenVPN on the same server. See chapters 13 and 16 for more details.

Next steps: Get your computer or device to use the VPN. Please refer to:

3.2 Configure IKEv2 VPN Clients (recommended)
5 Configure IPsec/L2TP VPN Clients
6 Configure IPsec/XAuth ("Cisco IPsec") VPN Clients

For other installation options, read the sections below.

▼ If you are unable to download, follow the steps below.

You may also use `curl` to download:

```
curl -fsSL https://get.vpnsetup.net -o vpn.sh && sudo sh vpn.sh
```

Alternative setup URLs:

```
https://github.com/hwdsl2/setup-ipsec-vpn/raw/master/vpnsetup.sh
https://gitlab.com/hwdsl2/setup-ipsec-vpn/-/raw/master/vpnsetup.sh
```

2.3 Requirements

A cloud server, virtual private server (VPS) or dedicated server, with an install of:

- Ubuntu Linux LTS
- Debian Linux
- CentOS or CentOS Stream
- Rocky Linux or AlmaLinux
- Oracle Linux
- Amazon Linux 2

▼ Other supported Linux distributions:

- Raspberry Pi OS (Raspbian)
- Kali Linux

- Alpine Linux
- Red Hat Enterprise Linux (RHEL)

This also includes Linux VMs in public clouds, such as DigitalOcean, Vultr, Linode, OVH and Microsoft Azure. For servers with an external firewall (e.g. EC2/GCE), open UDP ports 500 and 4500 for the VPN.

Quick deploy to:
DigitalOcean: http://dovpn.carlfriess.com
Linode: https://cloud.linode.com/stackscripts/37239

A pre-built Docker image is also available, see chapter 11 for more details. Advanced users can install on a Raspberry Pi. See:
https://stewright.me/2018/07/create-a-raspberry-pi-vpn-server-using-l2tpipsec/
https://elasticbyte.net/posts/setting-up-a-native-cisco-ipsec-vpn-server-using-a-raspberry-pi/

Warning: DO NOT run these scripts on your PC or Mac! They should only be used on a server!

2.4 Installation

First, update your server with `sudo apt-get update && sudo apt-get dist-upgrade` (Ubuntu/Debian) or `sudo yum update` and reboot. This is optional, but recommended.

To install the VPN, please choose one of the following options:

Option 1: Have the script generate random VPN credentials for you (will be displayed when finished).

```
wget https://get.vpnsetup.net -O vpn.sh && sudo sh vpn.sh
```

Option 2: Edit the script and provide your own VPN credentials.

```
wget https://get.vpnsetup.net -O vpn.sh
nano -w vpn.sh
[Replace with your own values: YOUR_IPSEC_PSK, YOUR_USERNAME and
```

```
YOUR_PASSWORD]
sudo sh vpn.sh
```

Note: A secure IPsec PSK should consist of at least 20 random characters.

Option 3: Define your VPN credentials as environment variables.

```
# All values MUST be placed inside 'single quotes'
# DO NOT use these special characters within values: \ " '
wget https://get.vpnsetup.net -O vpn.sh
sudo VPN_IPSEC_PSK='your_ipsec_pre_shared_key' \
VPN_USER='your_vpn_username' \
VPN_PASSWORD='your_vpn_password' \
sh vpn.sh
```

You may optionally install WireGuard and/or OpenVPN on the same server. See chapters 13 and 16 for more details. If your server runs CentOS Stream, Rocky Linux or AlmaLinux, first install OpenVPN/WireGuard, then install the IPsec VPN.

▼ If you are unable to download, follow the steps below.

You may also use `curl` to download. For example:

```
curl -fL https://get.vpnsetup.net -o vpn.sh && sudo sh vpn.sh
```

Alternative setup URLs:

```
https://github.com/hwdsl2/setup-ipsec-vpn/raw/master/vpnsetup.sh
https://gitlab.com/hwdsl2/setup-ipsec-vpn/-/raw/master/vpnsetup.sh
```

2.5 Next steps

Get your computer or device to use the VPN. Please refer to:

3.2 Configure IKEv2 VPN Clients (recommended)
5 Configure IPsec/L2TP VPN Clients
6 Configure IPsec/XAuth ("Cisco IPsec") VPN Clients

Enjoy your very own VPN!

2.6 Important notes

Windows users: For IPsec/L2TP mode, a one-time registry change is required if the VPN server or client is behind NAT (e.g. home router). See chapter 7, IPsec VPN: Troubleshooting, section 7.3.1.

The same VPN account can be used by your multiple devices. However, due to an IPsec/L2TP limitation, if you wish to connect multiple devices from behind the same NAT (e.g. home router), you must use IKEv2 or IPsec/XAuth mode. To view or update VPN user accounts, see chapter 9, IPsec VPN: Manage VPN Users.

For servers with an external firewall (e.g. EC2/GCE), open UDP ports 500 and 4500 for the VPN.

Clients are set to use Google Public DNS when the VPN is active. If another DNS provider is preferred, see chapter 8, IPsec VPN: Advanced Usage.

Using kernel support could improve IPsec/L2TP performance. It is available on all supported OS. Ubuntu users should install the `linux-modules-extra-$(uname -r)` package and run `service xl2tpd restart`.

The scripts will backup existing config files before making changes, with `.old-date-time` suffix.

2.7 Upgrade Libreswan

Use this one-liner to update Libreswan (https://libreswan.org) on your VPN server. Check installed version: `ipsec --version`.

```
wget https://get.vpnsetup.net/upg -O vpnup.sh && sudo sh vpnup.sh
```

Changelog: https://github.com/libreswan/libreswan/blob/main/CHANGES
Announce: https://lists.libreswan.org/mailman/listinfo/swan-announce

▼ If you are unable to download, follow the steps below.

You may also use `curl` to download:

```
curl -fsSL https://get.vpnsetup.net/upg -o vpnup.sh
sudo sh vpnup.sh
```

Alternative update URLs:

```
https://github.com/hwdsl2/setup-ipsec-
vpn/raw/master/extras/vpnupgrade.sh
https://gitlab.com/hwdsl2/setup-ipsec-
vpn/-/raw/master/extras/vpnupgrade.sh
```

Note: `xl2tpd` can be updated using your system's package manager, such as `apt-get` on Ubuntu/Debian.

2.8 Customize IKEv2 options

When installing the VPN, advanced users can optionally customize IKEv2 options.

▼ Option 1: Customize IKEv2 options using environment variables.

When installing the VPN, you can optionally specify a DNS name for the IKEv2 server address. The DNS name must be a fully qualified domain name (FQDN). Example:

```
sudo VPN_DNS_NAME='vpn.example.com' sh vpn.sh
```

Similarly, you may specify a name for the first IKEv2 client. The default is `vpnclient` if not specified.

```
sudo VPN_CLIENT_NAME='your_client_name' sh vpn.sh
```

By default, clients are set to use Google Public DNS when the VPN is active. You may specify custom DNS server(s) for all VPN modes. Example:

```
sudo VPN_DNS_SRV1=1.1.1.1 VPN_DNS_SRV2=1.0.0.1 sh vpn.sh
```

By default, no password is required when importing IKEv2 client configuration. You can choose to protect client config files using a random password.

```
sudo VPN_PROTECT_CONFIG=yes sh vpn.sh
```

▼ Option 2: Skip IKEv2 during VPN setup, then set up IKEv2 using custom options.

When installing the VPN, you can skip IKEv2 and only install the IPsec/L2TP and IPsec/XAuth ("Cisco IPsec") modes:

```
sudo VPN_SKIP_IKEV2=yes sh vpn.sh
```

(Optional) If you want to specify custom DNS server(s) for VPN clients, define VPN_DNS_SRV1 and optionally VPN_DNS_SRV2. Refer to option 1 above.

After that, run the IKEv2 helper script to set up IKEv2 interactively using custom options:

```
sudo ikev2.sh
```

Note: The VPN_SKIP_IKEV2 variable has no effect if IKEv2 is already set up on the server. In that case, to customize IKEv2 options, you can first remove IKEv2, then set it up again using sudo ikev2.sh.

▼ For reference: List of IKEv1 and IKEv2 parameters.

IKEv1 parameter*	Default value	Customize (env var)**
Server address (DNS name)	-	No, but you can connect using a DNS name
Server address (public IP)	Auto detect	VPN_PUBLIC_IP
IPsec pre-shared key	Auto generate	VPN_IPSEC_PSK
VPN username	vpnuser	VPN_USER
VPN password	Auto generate	VPN_PASSWORD
DNS servers for clients	Google Public DNS	VPN_DNS_SRV1, VPN_DNS_SRV2
Skip IKEv2 setup	no	VPN_SKIP_IKEV2=yes

* These IKEv1 parameters are for IPsec/L2TP and IPsec/XAuth ("Cisco IPsec") modes.
** Define these as environment variables when running vpn(setup).sh.

IKEv2 parameter*	Default value	Customize (env var)**	Customize (inter-active)***
Server address (DNS name)	-	VPN_DNS_NAME	✔
Server address (public IP)	Auto detect	VPN_PUBLIC_IP	✔
Name of first client	vpnclient	VPN_CLIENT_NAME	✔
DNS servers for clients	Google Public DNS	VPN_DNS_SRV1, VPN_DNS_SRV2	✔
Protect client config files	no	VPN_PROTECT_CONFIG =yes	✔
Enable/Disable MOBIKE	Enable if supported	✘	✔
Client cert validity****	10 years (120 months)	VPN_CLIENT_VALIDITY	✔
CA & server cert validity	10 years (120 months)	✘	✘
CA certificate name	IKEv2 VPN CA	✘	✘
Certificate key size	3072 bits	✘	✘

* These IKEv2 parameters are for IKEv2 mode.

** Define these as environment variables when running vpn(setup).sh, or when setting up IKEv2 in auto mode (sudo ikev2.sh --auto).

*** Can be customized during interactive IKEv2 setup (sudo ikev2.sh). Refer to option 2 above.

**** Use VPN_CLIENT_VALIDITY to specify the client cert validity period in months. Must be an integer between 1 and 120.

In addition to these parameters, advanced users can also customize VPN subnets during VPN setup. See chapter 8, IPsec VPN: Advanced Usage, section 8.5.

2.9 Uninstall the VPN

To uninstall IPsec VPN, run the helper script:

Warning: This helper script will remove IPsec VPN from your server. All VPN configuration will be **permanently deleted**, and Libreswan and xl2tpd will be removed. This **cannot be undone**!

```
wget https://get.vpnsetup.net/unst -O unst.sh && sudo bash unst.sh
```

▼ If you are unable to download, follow the steps below.

You may also use `curl` to download:

```
curl -fsSL https://get.vpnsetup.net/unst -o unst.sh
sudo bash unst.sh
```

Alternative script URLs:

```
https://github.com/hwdsl2/setup-ipsec-
vpn/raw/master/extras/vpnuninstall.sh
https://gitlab.com/hwdsl2/setup-ipsec-
vpn/-/raw/master/extras/vpnuninstall.sh
```

For more information, see chapter 10, IPsec VPN: Uninstall the VPN.

3 Guide: How to Set Up and Use IKEv2 VPN

- Introduction
- Configure IKEv2 VPN clients
- Manage IKEv2 clients
- Change IKEv2 server address
- Update IKEv2 helper script
- Set up IKEv2 using helper script
- Manually set up IKEv2
- Remove IKEv2

3.1 Introduction

Modern operating systems support the IKEv2 standard. Internet Key Exchange (IKE or IKEv2) is the protocol used to set up a Security Association (SA) in the IPsec protocol suite. Compared to IKE version 1, IKEv2 contains improvements such as Standard Mobility support through MOBIKE, and improved reliability.

Libreswan can authenticate IKEv2 clients on the basis of X.509 Machine Certificates using RSA signatures. This method does not require an IPsec PSK, username or password. It can be used with Windows, macOS, iOS, Android, Chrome OS and Linux.

By default, IKEv2 is automatically set up when running the VPN setup script. If you want to learn more about setting up IKEv2, see section 3.6 Set up IKEv2 using helper script. Docker users, see section 11.9 Configure and use IKEv2 VPN.

3.2 Configure IKEv2 VPN clients

Note: To add or export IKEv2 clients, run `sudo ikev2.sh`. Use `-h` to show usage. Client config files can be safely deleted after import.

- Windows 7, 8, 10 and 11
- OS X (macOS)
- iOS (iPhone/iPad)
- Android
- Chrome OS (Chromebook)
- Linux

▼ Learn how to change the IKEv2 server address.

In certain circumstances, you may need to change the IKEv2 server address. For example, to switch to use a DNS name, or after server IP changes. Learn more in section 3.4 Change IKEv2 server address.

3.2.1 Windows 7, 8, 10 and 11

3.2.1.1 Auto-import configuration

Screencast: IKEv2 Auto Import Configuration on Windows
https://youtu.be/H8-S35OgoeE

Windows 8, 10 and 11 users can automatically import IKEv2 configuration:

1. Securely transfer the generated `.p12` file to your computer.
2. Download ikev2_config_import.cmd (https://github.com/hwdsl2/vpn-extras/releases/latest/download/ikev2_config_import.cmd) and save this helper script to the **same folder** as the `.p12` file.
3. Right-click on the saved script, select **Properties**. Click on **Unblock** at the bottom, then click on **OK**.
4. Right-click on the saved script, select **Run as administrator** and follow the prompts.

To connect to the VPN: Click on the wireless/network icon in your system tray, select the new VPN entry, and click **Connect**. Once connected, you can verify that your traffic is being routed properly by looking up your IP address on Google. It should say "Your public IP address is `Your VPN Server IP`".

If you get an error when trying to connect, see section 7.2 IKEv2 troubleshooting.

3.2.1.2 Manually import configuration

Screencast: IKEv2 Manually Import Configuration on Windows 8/10/11
https://youtu.be/-CDnvh58EJM
Screencast: IKEv2 Manually Import Configuration on Windows 7
https://youtu.be/UsBWmO-CRCo

Alternatively, **Windows 7, 8, 10 and 11** users can manually import IKEv2 configuration:

1. Securely transfer the generated .p12 file to your computer, then import it into the certificate store.

   To import the .p12 file, run the following from an elevated command prompt:

   ```
   # Import .p12 file (replace with your own value)
   certutil -f -importpfx "\path\to\your\file.p12" NoExport
   ```

   Note: If there is no password for client config files, press Enter to continue, or if manually importing the .p12 file, leave the password field blank.

   Alternatively, you can manually import the .p12 file:
   https://wiki.strongswan.org/projects/strongswan/wiki/Win7Certs/9

   Make sure that the client cert is placed in "Personal -> Certificates", and the CA cert is placed in "Trusted Root Certification Authorities -> Certificates".

2. On the Windows computer, add a new IKEv2 VPN connection.

   For **Windows 8, 10 and 11**, it is recommended to create the VPN connection using the following commands from a command prompt, for improved security and performance.

   ```
   # Create VPN connection (replace server address
   # with your own value)
   powershell -command ^"Add-VpnConnection ^
     -ServerAddress 'Your VPN Server IP (or DNS name)' ^
     -Name 'My IKEv2 VPN' -TunnelType IKEv2 ^
   ```

17

```
    —AuthenticationMethod MachineCertificate ^
    —EncryptionLevel Required —PassThru^"
  # Set IPsec configuration
  powershell —command ^"Set-VpnConnectionIPsecConfiguration ^
    —ConnectionName 'My IKEv2 VPN' ^
    —AuthenticationTransformConstants GCMAES128 ^
    —CipherTransformConstants GCMAES128 ^
    —EncryptionMethod AES256 ^
    —IntegrityCheckMethod SHA256 —PfsGroup None ^
    —DHGroup Group14 —PassThru —Force^"
```

Windows 7 does not support these commands, you can manually create the VPN connection:

https://wiki.strongswan.org/projects/strongswan/wiki/Win7Config/8

Note: The server address you specify must **exactly match** the server address in the output of the IKEv2 helper script. For example, if you specified the server's DNS name during IKEv2 setup, you must enter the DNS name in the **Internet address** field.

3. **This step is required if you manually created the VPN connection.**

   Enable stronger ciphers for IKEv2 with a one-time registry change. Run the following from an elevated command prompt.

   ◦ For Windows 7, 8, 10 and 11

```
REG ADD HKLM\SYSTEM\CurrentControlSet\Services\RasMan\Parameters ^
 /v NegotiateDH2048_AES256 /t REG_DWORD /d 0x1 /f
```

To connect to the VPN: Click on the wireless/network icon in your system tray, select the new VPN entry, and click **Connect**. Once connected, you can verify that your traffic is being routed properly by looking up your IP address on Google. It should say "Your public IP address is `Your VPN Server IP`".

If you get an error when trying to connect, see section 7.2 IKEv2 troubleshooting.

▼ Remove the IKEv2 VPN connection.

Using the following steps, you can remove the VPN connection and optionally restore the computer to the status before IKEv2 configuration import.

1. Remove the added VPN connection in Windows Settings - Network - VPN. Windows 7 users can remove the VPN connection in Network and Sharing Center - Change adapter settings.

2. (Optional) Remove IKEv2 certificates.

    1. Press Win+R, or search for `mmc` in the Start Menu. Open *Microsoft Management Console*.

    2. Open `File` - `Add/Remove Snap-In`. Select to add `Certificates` and in the window that opens, select `Computer account` -> `Local Computer`. Click on `Finish` -> `OK` to save the settings.

    3. Go to `Certificates` - `Personal` - `Certificates` and delete the IKEv2 client certificate. The name of the certificate is the same as the IKEv2 client name you specified (default: `vpnclient`). The certificate was issued by `IKEv2 VPN CA`.

    4. Go to `Certificates` - `Trusted Root Certification Authorities` - `Certificates` and delete the IKEv2 VPN CA certificate. The certificate was issued to `IKEv2 VPN CA` by `IKEv2 VPN CA`. Before deleting, make sure that there are no other certificate(s) issued by `IKEv2 VPN CA` in `Certificates` - `Personal` - `Certificates`.

3. (Optional. For users who manually created the VPN connection) Restore registry settings. Note that you should backup the registry before editing.

    1. Press Win+R, or search for `regedit` in the Start Menu. Open *Registry Editor*.

    2. Go to:
    `HKEY_LOCAL_MACHINE\System\CurrentControlSet\Services\Rasman\Parameters` and delete the item with name `NegotiateDH2048_AES256`, if it exists.

3.2.2 OS X (macOS)

Screencast: IKEv2 Import Configuration and Connect on macOS
https://youtu.be/E2IZMUtR7kU

First, securely transfer the generated `.mobileconfig` file to your Mac, then double-click and follow the prompts to import as a macOS profile. If your Mac runs macOS Big Sur or newer, open System Preferences and go to the Profiles section to finish importing. For macOS Ventura and newer, open System Settings and search for Profiles. When finished, check to make sure "IKEv2 VPN" is listed under System Preferences -> Profiles.

To connect to the VPN:

1. Open System Preferences and go to the Network section.
2. Select the VPN connection with `Your VPN Server IP` (or DNS name).
3. Check the **Show VPN status in menu bar** checkbox. For macOS Ventura and newer, this setting can be configured in System Settings -> Control Center -> Menu Bar Only section.
4. Click **Connect**, or slide the VPN switch ON.

(Optional feature) Enable **VPN On Demand** to automatically start a VPN connection when your Mac is on Wi-Fi. To enable, check the **Connect on demand** checkbox for the VPN connection, and click **Apply**. To find this setting on macOS Ventura and newer, click on the "i" icon on the right of the VPN connection.

You can customize VPN On Demand rules to exclude certain Wi-Fi network(s) such as your home network. See chapter 4, Guide: Customize IKEv2 VPN On Demand Rules for macOS and iOS.

▼ If you manually set up IKEv2 without using the VPN script, follow the steps below.

First, securely transfer the generated `.p12` file to your Mac, then double-click to import into the **login** keychain in **Keychain Access**. Next, double-click on the imported `IKEv2 VPN CA` certificate, expand **Trust** and select **Always Trust** from the **IP Security (IPsec)** drop-down menu. Close the dialog using the red "X" on the top-left corner. When prompted, use Touch ID or enter your password and click "Update Settings".

When finished, check to make sure both the new client certificate and IKEv2 VPN CA are listed under the **Certificates** category of **login** keychain.

1. Open System Preferences and go to the Network section.
2. Click the + button in the lower-left corner of the window.
3. Select **VPN** from the **Interface** drop-down menu.
4. Select **IKEv2** from the **VPN Type** drop-down menu.
5. Enter anything you like for the **Service Name**.
6. Click **Create**.
7. Enter Your VPN Server IP (or DNS name) for the **Server Address**.
   Note: If you specified the server's DNS name (instead of its IP address) during IKEv2 setup, you must enter the DNS name in the **Server Address** and **Remote ID** fields.
8. Enter Your VPN Server IP (or DNS name) for the **Remote ID**.
9. Enter Your VPN client name in the **Local ID** field.
   Note: This must match exactly the client name you specified during IKEv2 setup. Same as the first part of your .p12 filename.
10. Click the **Authentication Settings...** button.
11. Select **None** from the **Authentication Settings** drop-down menu.
12. Select the **Certificate** radio button, then select the new client certificate.
13. Click **OK**.
14. Check the **Show VPN status in menu bar** checkbox.
15. Click **Apply** to save the VPN connection information.
16. Click **Connect**.

Once connected, you can verify that your traffic is being routed properly by looking up your IP address on Google. It should say "Your public IP address is Your VPN Server IP".

If you get an error when trying to connect, see section 7.2 IKEv2 troubleshooting.

▼ Remove the IKEv2 VPN connection.

To remove the IKEv2 VPN connection, open System Preferences -> Profiles and remove the IKEv2 VPN profile you added.

3.2.3 iOS

Screencast: IKEv2 Import Configuration and Connect on iOS (iPhone & iPad)
https://youtube.com/shorts/Y5HuX7jk_Kc

First, securely transfer the generated `.mobileconfig` file to your iOS device, then import it as an iOS profile. To transfer the file, you may use:

1. AirDrop, or
2. Upload to your device (any App folder) using File Sharing (https://support.apple.com/en-us/HT210598), then open the "Files" App on your iOS device, move the uploaded file to the "On My iPhone" folder. After that, tap the file and go to the "Settings" App to import, or
3. Host the file on a secure website of yours, then download and import it in Mobile Safari.

When finished, check to make sure "IKEv2 VPN" is listed under Settings -> General -> VPN & Device Management or Profile(s).

To connect to the VPN:

1. Go to Settings -> VPN. Select the VPN connection with `Your VPN Server IP` (or DNS name).
2. Slide the **VPN** switch ON.

(Optional feature) Enable **VPN On Demand** to automatically start a VPN connection when your iOS device is on Wi-Fi. To enable, tap the "i" icon on the right of the VPN connection, and enable **Connect On Demand**.

You can customize VPN On Demand rules to exclude certain Wi-Fi network(s) such as your home network, or to start the VPN connection both on Wi-Fi and cellular. See chapter 4, Guide: Customize IKEv2 VPN On Demand Rules for macOS and iOS.

▼ If you manually set up IKEv2 without using the VPN script, follow the steps below.

First, securely transfer the generated `ca.cer` and `.p12` files to your iOS device, then import them one by one as iOS profiles. To transfer the files, you may use:

1. AirDrop, or
2. Upload to your device (any App folder) using File Sharing (https://support.apple.com/en-us/HT210598), then open the "Files" App on your iOS device, move the uploaded files to the "On My iPhone" folder. After that, tap each file and go to the "Settings" App to import, or
3. Host the files on a secure website of yours, then download and import them in Mobile Safari.

When finished, check to make sure both the new client certificate and `IKEv2 VPN CA` are listed under Settings -> General -> VPN & Device Management or Profile(s).

1. Go to Settings -> General -> VPN & Device Management -> VPN.
2. Tap **Add VPN Configuration...**.
3. Tap **Type**. Select **IKEv2** and go back.
4. Tap **Description** and enter anything you like.
5. Tap **Server** and enter `Your VPN Server IP` (or DNS name).
   Note: If you specified the server's DNS name (instead of its IP address) during IKEv2 setup, you must enter the DNS name in the **Server** and **Remote ID** fields.
6. Tap **Remote ID** and enter `Your VPN Server IP` (or DNS name).
7. Enter `Your VPN client name` in the **Local ID** field.
   Note: This must match exactly the client name you specified during IKEv2 setup. Same as the first part of your `.p12` filename.
8. Tap **User Authentication**. Select **None** and go back.
9. Make sure the **Use Certificate** switch is ON.
10. Tap **Certificate**. Select the new client certificate and go back.
11. Tap **Done**.
12. Slide the **VPN** switch ON.

Once connected, you can verify that your traffic is being routed properly by looking up your IP address on Google. It should say "Your public IP address is `Your VPN Server IP`".

If you get an error when trying to connect, see section 7.2 IKEv2 troubleshooting.

▼ Remove the IKEv2 VPN connection.

To remove the IKEv2 VPN connection, open Settings -> General -> VPN & Device Management or Profile(s) and remove the IKEv2 VPN profile you added.

3.2.4 Android

Screencast: Connect using Android strongSwan VPN Client
https://youtu.be/i6j1N_7cI-w

1. Securely transfer the generated .sswan file to your Android device.
2. Install strongSwan VPN Client from **Google Play**.
3. Launch the strongSwan VPN client.
4. Tap the "more options" menu on top right, then tap **Import VPN profile**.
5. Choose the .sswan file you transferred from the VPN server.
   Note: To find the .sswan file, tap the three-line menu button, then browse to the location you saved the file.
6. On the "Import VPN profile" screen, tap **Import certificate from VPN profile**, and follow the prompts.
7. On the "Choose certificate" screen, select the new client certificate, then tap **Select**.
8. Tap **Import**.
9. Tap the new VPN profile to connect.

▼ Alternatively, Android 11+ users can also connect using the native IKEv2 client.

Screencast: Connect using Native VPN Client on Android 11+
https://youtu.be/Cai6k4GgkEE

1. Securely transfer the generated .p12 file to your Android device.
2. Launch the **Settings** application.
3. Go to Security -> Advanced -> Encryption & credentials.
4. Tap **Install a certificate**.

5. Tap **VPN & app user certificate**.

6. Choose the .p12 file you transferred from the VPN server.
   Note: To find the .p12 file, tap the three-line menu button, then browse to the location you saved the file.

7. Enter a name for the certificate, then tap **OK**.

8. Go to Settings -> Network & internet -> VPN, then tap the "+" button.

9. Enter a name for the VPN profile.

10. Select **IKEv2/IPSec RSA** from the **Type** drop-down menu.

11. Enter Your VPN Server IP (or DNS name) in the **Server address** field.
    Note: This must **exactly match** the server address in the output of the IKEv2 helper script.

12. Enter anything (e.g. empty) in the **IPSec identifier** field.
    Note: This field should not be required. It is a bug in Android.

13. Select the certificate you imported from the **IPSec user certificate** drop-down menu.

14. Select the certificate you imported from the **IPSec CA certificate** drop-down menu.

15. Select **(receive from server)** from the **IPSec server certificate** drop-down menu.

16. Tap **Save**. Then tap the new VPN connection and tap **Connect**.

If your device runs Android 6.0 (Marshmallow) or older, in order to connect using the strongSwan VPN client, you must make the following change on the VPN server: Edit /etc/ipsec.d/ikev2.conf on the server. Append authby=rsa-sha1 to the end of the conn ikev2-cp section, indented by two spaces. Save the file and run service ipsec restart.

(Optional feature) You can choose to enable the "Always-on VPN" feature on Android. Launch the **Settings** app, go to Network & internet -> Advanced -> VPN, click the gear icon on the right of "strongSwan VPN Client", then enable the **Always-on VPN** and **Block connections without VPN** options.

▼ If you manually set up IKEv2 without using the VPN script, follow the steps below.

Android 10 and newer:

1. Securely transfer the generated .p12 file to your Android device.

2. Install strongSwan VPN Client from **Google Play**.
3. Launch the **Settings** application.
4. Go to Security -> Advanced -> Encryption & credentials.
5. Tap **Install a certificate**.
6. Tap **VPN & app user certificate**.
7. Choose the `.p12` file you transferred from the VPN server, and follow the prompts.
   Note: To find the `.p12` file, tap the three-line menu button, then browse to the location you saved the file.
8. Launch the strongSwan VPN client and tap **Add VPN Profile**.
9. Enter `Your VPN Server IP` (or DNS name) in the **Server** field.
   Note: If you specified the server's DNS name (instead of its IP address) during IKEv2 setup, you must enter the DNS name in the **Server** field.
10. Select **IKEv2 Certificate** from the **VPN Type** drop-down menu.
11. Tap **Select user certificate**, select the new client certificate and confirm.
12. **(Important)** Tap **Show advanced settings**. Scroll down, find and enable the **Use RSA/PSS signatures** option.
13. Save the new VPN connection, then tap to connect.

Android 4 to 9:

1. Securely transfer the generated `.p12` file to your Android device.
2. Install strongSwan VPN Client from **Google Play**.
3. Launch the strongSwan VPN client and tap **Add VPN Profile**.
4. Enter `Your VPN Server IP` (or DNS name) in the **Server** field.
   Note: If you specified the server's DNS name (instead of its IP address) during IKEv2 setup, you must enter the DNS name in the **Server** field.
5. Select **IKEv2 Certificate** from the **VPN Type** drop-down menu.
6. Tap **Select user certificate**, then tap **Install certificate**.
7. Choose the `.p12` file you transferred from the VPN server, and follow the prompts.
   Note: To find the `.p12` file, tap the three-line menu button, then browse to the location you saved the file.
8. **(Important)** Tap **Show advanced settings**. Scroll down, find and enable the **Use RSA/PSS signatures** option.
9. Save the new VPN connection, then tap to connect.

Once connected, you can verify that your traffic is being routed properly by looking up your IP address on Google. It should say "Your public IP address is Your VPN Server IP".

If you get an error when trying to connect, see section 7.2 IKEv2 troubleshooting.

3.2.5 Chrome OS

First, on your VPN server, export the CA certificate as `ca.cer`:

```
sudo certutil -L -d sql:/etc/ipsec.d \
  -n "IKEv2 VPN CA" -a -o ca.cer
```

Securely transfer the generated `.p12` and `ca.cer` files to your Chrome OS device.

Install user and CA certificates:

1. Open a new tab in Google Chrome.
2. In the address bar, enter **chrome://settings/certificates**
3. **(Important)** Click **Import and Bind**, not **Import**.
4. In the box that opens, choose the `.p12` file you transferred from the VPN server and select **Open**.
5. Click **OK** if the certificate does not have a password. Otherwise, enter the certificate's password.
6. Click the **Authorities** tab. Then click **Import**.
7. In the box that opens, select **All files** in the drop-down menu at the bottom left.
8. Choose the `ca.cer` file you transferred from the VPN server and select **Open**.
9. Keep the default options and click **OK**.

Add a new VPN connection:

1. Go to Settings -> Network.
2. Click **Add connection**, then click **Add built-in VPN**.
3. Enter anything you like for the **Service name**.
4. Select **IPsec (IKEv2)** in the **Provider type** drop-down menu.
5. Enter Your VPN Server IP (or DNS name) for the **Server hostname**.

6. Select **User certificate** in the **Authentication type** drop-down menu.
7. Select **IKEv2 VPN CA [IKEv2 VPN CA]** in the **Server CA certificate** drop-down menu.
8. Select **IKEv2 VPN CA [client name]** in the **User certificate** drop-down menu.
9. Leave other fields blank.
10. Enable **Save identity and password**.
11. Click **Connect**.

Once connected, you will see a VPN icon overlay on the network status icon. You can verify that your traffic is being routed properly by looking up your IP address on Google. It should say "Your public IP address is Your VPN Server IP".

(Optional feature) You can choose to enable the "Always-on VPN" feature on Chrome OS. To manage this setting, go to Settings -> Network, then click **VPN**.

If you get an error when trying to connect, see section 7.2 IKEv2 troubleshooting.

3.2.6 Linux

Before configuring Linux VPN clients, you must make the following change on the VPN server: Edit `/etc/ipsec.d/ikev2.conf` on the server. Append `authby=rsa-sha1` to the end of the `conn ikev2-cp` section, indented by two spaces. Save the file and run `service ipsec restart`.

To configure your Linux computer to connect to IKEv2 as a VPN client, first install the strongSwan plugin for NetworkManager:

```
# Ubuntu and Debian
sudo apt-get update
sudo apt-get install network-manager-strongswan


# Arch Linux
sudo pacman -Syu  # upgrade all packages
sudo pacman -S networkmanager-strongswan
```

28

```
# Fedora
sudo yum install NetworkManager-strongswan-gnome


# CentOS
sudo yum install epel-release
sudo yum --enablerepo=epel install NetworkManager-strongswan-gnome
```

Next, securely transfer the generated .p12 file from the VPN server to your Linux computer. After that, extract the CA certificate, client certificate and private key. Replace vpnclient.p12 in the example below with the name of your .p12 file.

```
# Example: Extract CA certificate, client certificate
#          and private key. You may delete the .p12 file
#          when finished.
# Note: You may need to enter the import password,
#       which can be found in the output of the IKEv2
#       helper script. If the output does not contain
#       an import password, press Enter to continue.
# Note: If using OpenSSL 3.x (run "openssl version" to check),
#       append "-legacy" to the 3 commands below.
openssl pkcs12 -in vpnclient.p12 -cacerts -nokeys -out ca.cer
openssl pkcs12 -in vpnclient.p12 -clcerts -nokeys -out client.cer
openssl pkcs12 -in vpnclient.p12 -nocerts -nodes  -out client.key
rm vpnclient.p12


# (Important) Protect certificate and private key files
# Note: This step is optional, but strongly recommended.
sudo chown root.root ca.cer client.cer client.key
sudo chmod 600 ca.cer client.cer client.key
```

You can then set up and enable the VPN connection:

1. Go to Settings -> Network -> VPN. Click the + button.
2. Select **IPsec/IKEv2 (strongswan)**.
3. Enter anything you like in the **Name** field.
4. In the **Gateway (Server)** section, enter Your VPN Server IP (or DNS name) for the **Address**.
5. Select the ca.cer file for the **Certificate**.

6. In the **Client** section, select **Certificate(/private key)** in the **Authentication** drop-down menu.
7. Select **Certificate/private key** in the **Certificate** drop-down menu (if exists).
8. Select the `client.cer` file for the **Certificate (file)**.
9. Select the `client.key` file for the **Private key**.
10. In the **Options** section, check the **Request an inner IP address** checkbox.
11. In the **Cipher proposals (Algorithms)** section, check the **Enable custom proposals** checkbox.
12. Leave the **IKE** field blank.
13. Enter `aes128gcm16` in the **ESP** field.
14. Click **Add** to save the VPN connection information.
15. Turn the **VPN** switch ON.

Alternatively, you may connect using the command line. See the following links for example steps:

https://github.com/hwdsl2/setup-ipsec-vpn/issues/1399

https://github.com/hwdsl2/setup-ipsec-vpn/issues/1007

If you encounter error `Could not find source connection`, edit `/etc/netplan/01-netcfg.yaml` and replace `renderer: networkd` with `renderer: NetworkManager`, then run `sudo netplan apply`. To connect to the VPN, run `sudo nmcli c up VPN`. To disconnect: `sudo nmcli c down VPN`.

Once connected, you can verify that your traffic is being routed properly by looking up your IP address on Google. It should say "Your public IP address is `Your VPN Server IP`".

If you get an error when trying to connect, see section 7.2 IKEv2 troubleshooting.

3.3 Manage IKEv2 clients

After setting up the VPN server, you can manage IKEv2 VPN clients by following the instructions in this section. For example, you can add new IKEv2 client(s) on the server for your additional computers and mobile devices, list existing clients, or export configuration for an existing client.

To manage IKEv2 clients, first connect to your VPN server using SSH, then run:

```
sudo ikev2.sh
```

You will see the following options:

```
IKEv2 is already set up on this server.

Select an option:
  1) Add a new client
  2) Export config for an existing client
  3) List existing clients
  4) Revoke an existing client
  5) Delete an existing client
  6) Remove IKEv2
  7) Exit
Option:
```

You can then enter your desired option to manage IKEv2 clients.

Note: These options may change in newer versions of the script. Read carefully before selecting your desired option.

Alternatively, you may run `ikev2.sh` with command-line options. See below for details.

3.3.1 Add a new IKEv2 client

To add a new IKEv2 client:

1. Select option 1 from the menu, by typing 1 and pressing enter.
2. Provide a name for the new client.
3. Specify the validity period for the new client certificate.

Alternatively, you may run `ikev2.sh` with the `--addclient` option. Use option –h to show usage.

```
sudo ikev2.sh --addclient [client name]
```

Next steps: Configure IKEv2 VPN clients. See section 3.2 for more details.

3.3.2 Export an existing client

To export IKEv2 configuration for an existing client:

1. Select option 2 from the menu, by typing 2 and pressing enter.
2. From the list of existing clients, enter the name of the client you want to export.

Alternatively, you may run `ikev2.sh` with the `--exportclient` option.

```
sudo ikev2.sh --exportclient [client name]
```

3.3.3 List existing clients

Select option 3 from the menu, by typing 3 and pressing enter. The script will then display a list of existing IKEv2 clients.

Alternatively, you may run `ikev2.sh` with the `--listclients` option.

```
sudo ikev2.sh --listclients
```

3.3.4 Revoke an IKEv2 client

In certain circumstances, you may need to revoke a previously generated IKEv2 client certificate.

1. Select option 4 from the menu, by typing 4 and pressing enter.
2. From the list of existing clients, enter the name of the client you want to revoke.
3. Confirm the client revocation.

Alternatively, you may run `ikev2.sh` with the `--revokeclient` option.

```
sudo ikev2.sh --revokeclient [client name]
```

Alternatively, you can manually revoke a client certificate. This can be done using `crlutil`. See example steps below, commands must be run as `root`.

1. Check the database, and identify the nickname of the client certificate you want to revoke.

```
certutil -L -d sql:/etc/ipsec.d
```

```
Certificate Nickname    Trust Attributes
                        SSL,S/MIME,JAR/XPI


IKEv2 VPN CA            CTu,u,u
($PUBLIC_IP)           u,u,u
vpnclient-to-revoke    u,u,u
```

In this example, we will revoke the certificate with nickname vpnclient-to-revoke, issued by IKEv2 VPN CA.

2. Find the serial number of this client certificate.

```
certutil -L -d sql:/etc/ipsec.d -n "vpnclient-to-revoke"
```

```
Certificate:
    Data:
        Version: 3 (0x2)
        Serial Number:
            00:cd:69:ff:74
... ...
```

From the output, we see that the serial number is CD69FF74 in hexadecimal, which is 3446275956 in decimal. It will be used in the next steps.

3. Create a new Certificate Revocation List (CRL). You only need to do this once for each CA.

```
if ! crlutil -L -d sql:/etc/ipsec.d \
  -n "IKEv2 VPN CA" 2>/dev/null; then
  crlutil -G -d sql:/etc/ipsec.d -n "IKEv2 VPN CA" -c /dev/null
fi
```

```
CRL Info:
:
    Version: 2 (0x1)
    Signature Algorithm: PKCS #1 SHA-256 With RSA Encryption
    Issuer: "O=IKEv2 VPN,CN=IKEv2 VPN CA"
```

```
This Update: Sat Jun 06 22:00:00 2020
CRL Extensions:
```

4. Add the client certificate you want to revoke to the CRL. Here we specify the certificate's serial number in decimal, and the revocation time in GeneralizedTime format (YYYYMMDDhhmmssZ) in UTC.

```
crlutil -M -d sql:/etc/ipsec.d -n "IKEv2 VPN CA" <<EOF
addcert 3446275956 20200606220100Z
EOF

CRL Info:
:
    Version: 2 (0x1)
    Signature Algorithm: PKCS #1 SHA-256 With RSA Encryption
    Issuer: "O=IKEv2 VPN,CN=IKEv2 VPN CA"
    This Update: Sat Jun 06 22:02:00 2020
    Entry 1 (0x1):
        Serial Number:
            00:cd:69:ff:74
        Revocation Date: Sat Jun 06 22:01:00 2020
    CRL Extensions:
```

Note: If you want to remove a certificate from the CRL, replace `addcert 3446275956 20200606220100Z` above with `rmcert 3446275956`.

5. Finally, let Libreswan re-read the updated CRL.

```
ipsec crls
```

3.3.5 Delete an IKEv2 client

Important: Deleting a client certificate from the IPsec database **will not** prevent VPN client(s) from connecting using that certificate! For this use case, you **must** revoke the client certificate instead of deleting it.

Warning: The client certificate and private key will be **permanently deleted**. This **cannot be undone**!

To delete an existing IKEv2 client:

1. Select option 5 from the menu, by typing 5 and pressing enter.
2. From the list of existing clients, enter the name of the client you want to delete.
3. Confirm the client deletion.

Alternatively, you may run `ikev2.sh` with the `--deleteclient` option.

```
sudo ikev2.sh --deleteclient [client name]
```

▼ Alternatively, you can manually delete a client certificate.

1. List certificates in the IPsec database:

   ```
   certutil -L -d sql:/etc/ipsec.d
   ```

   Example output:

   ```
   Certificate Nickname    Trust Attributes
                           SSL,S/MIME,JAR/XPI

   IKEv2 VPN CA            CTu,u,u
   ($PUBLIC_IP)            u,u,u
   vpnclient              u,u,u
   ```

2. Delete the client certificate and private key. Replace "Nickname" below with the nickname of the client certificate you want to delete, e.g. vpnclient.

   ```
   certutil -F -d sql:/etc/ipsec.d -n "Nickname"
   certutil -D -d sql:/etc/ipsec.d -n "Nickname" 2>/dev/null
   ```

3. (Optional) Delete the previously generated client configuration files (`.p12`, `.mobileconfig` and `.sswan` files) for this VPN client, if any.

3.4 Change IKEv2 server address

In certain circumstances, you may need to change the IKEv2 server address after setup. For example, to switch to use a DNS name, or after server IP changes. Note that the server address you specify on VPN client devices must

exactly match the server address in the output of the IKEv2 helper script. Otherwise, devices may be unable to connect.

To change the server address, run the helper script and follow the prompts.

```
wget https://get.vpnsetup.net/ikev2addr -O ikev2addr.sh
sudo bash ikev2addr.sh
```

Important: After running this script, you must manually update the server address (and remote ID, if applicable) on any existing IKEv2 client devices. For iOS clients, you'll need to export and re-import client configuration using the IKEv2 helper script.

3.5 Update IKEv2 helper script

The IKEv2 helper script is updated from time to time for bug fixes and improvements. See the following link for commit log:
https://github.com/hwdsl2/setup-ipsec-vpn/commits/master/extras/ikev2setup.sh

When a newer version is available, you may optionally update the IKEv2 helper script on your server. Note that these commands will overwrite any existing ikev2.sh.

```
wget https://get.vpnsetup.net/ikev2 -O /opt/src/ikev2.sh
chmod +x /opt/src/ikev2.sh \
  && ln -s /opt/src/ikev2.sh /usr/bin 2>/dev/null
```

3.6 Set up IKEv2 using helper script

Note: By default, IKEv2 is automatically set up when running the VPN setup script. You may skip this section and continue to section 3.2 Configure IKEv2 VPN clients.

Important: Before continuing, you should have successfully set up your own VPN server. Docker users, see section 11.9 Configure and use IKEv2 VPN.

Use this helper script to automatically set up IKEv2 on the VPN server:

```
# Set up IKEv2 using default options
sudo ikev2.sh --auto
# Alternatively, you may customize IKEv2 options
sudo ikev2.sh
```

Note: If IKEv2 is already set up, but you want to customize IKEv2 options, first remove IKEv2, then set it up again using `sudo ikev2.sh`.

When finished, continue to section 3.2 Configure IKEv2 VPN clients. Advanced users can optionally enable IKEv2-only mode. See section 8.3 for more details.

▼ You may optionally specify a DNS name, client name and/or custom DNS servers.

When running IKEv2 setup in auto mode, advanced users can optionally specify a DNS name for the IKEv2 server address. The DNS name must be a fully qualified domain name (FQDN). Example:

```
sudo VPN_DNS_NAME='vpn.example.com' ikev2.sh --auto
```

Similarly, you may specify a name for the first IKEv2 client. The default is `vpnclient` if not specified.

```
sudo VPN_CLIENT_NAME='your_client_name' ikev2.sh --auto
```

By default, IKEv2 clients are set to use Google Public DNS when the VPN is active. You may specify custom DNS server(s) for IKEv2. Example:

```
sudo VPN_DNS_SRV1=1.1.1.1 VPN_DNS_SRV2=1.0.0.1 ikev2.sh --auto
```

By default, no password is required when importing IKEv2 client configuration. You can choose to protect client config files using a random password.

```
sudo VPN_PROTECT_CONFIG=yes ikev2.sh --auto
```

To view usage information for the IKEv2 script, run `sudo ikev2.sh -h` on your server.

3.7 Manually set up IKEv2

As an alternative to using the helper script, advanced users can manually set up IKEv2 on the VPN server. Before continuing, it is recommended to update Libreswan to the latest version (see section 2.7).

View example steps for manually setting up IKEv2:
https://github.com/hwdsl2/setup-ipsec-vpn/blob/master/docs/ikev2-howto.md#manually-set-up-ikev2

3.8 Remove IKEv2

If you want to remove IKEv2 from the VPN server, but keep the IPsec/L2TP and IPsec/XAuth ("Cisco IPsec") modes (if installed), run the helper script. **Warning:** All IKEv2 configuration including certificates and keys will be **permanently deleted**. This **cannot be undone**!

```
sudo ikev2.sh --removeikev2
```

After removing IKEv2, if you want to set it up again, refer to section 3.6 Set up IKEv2 using helper script.

▼ Alternatively, you can manually remove IKEv2.

To manually remove IKEv2 from the VPN server, but keep the IPsec/L2TP and IPsec/XAuth ("Cisco IPsec") modes, follow these steps. Commands must be run as root.

Warning: All IKEv2 configuration including certificates and keys will be **permanently deleted**. This **cannot be undone**!

1. Rename (or delete) the IKEv2 config file:

   ```
   mv /etc/ipsec.d/ikev2.conf /etc/ipsec.d/ikev2.conf.bak
   ```

2. **(Important) Restart the IPsec service**:

   ```
   service ipsec restart
   ```

3. List certificates in the IPsec database:

```
certutil -L -d sql:/etc/ipsec.d
```

Example output:

```
Certificate Nickname   Trust Attributes
                       SSL,S/MIME,JAR/XPI


IKEv2 VPN CA           CTu,u,u
($PUBLIC_IP)           u,u,u
vpnclient              u,u,u
```

4. Delete the Certificate Revocation List (CRL), if any:

```
crlutil -D -d sql:/etc/ipsec.d -n "IKEv2 VPN CA" 2>/dev/null
```

5. Delete certificates and keys. Replace "Nickname" below with each certificate's nickname. Repeat these commands for each certificate. When finished, list certificates in the IPsec database again, and confirm that the list is empty.

```
certutil -F -d sql:/etc/ipsec.d -n "Nickname"
certutil -D -d sql:/etc/ipsec.d -n "Nickname" 2>/dev/null
```

4 Guide: Customize IKEv2 VPN On Demand Rules for macOS and iOS

4.1 Introduction

VPN On Demand is an optional feature on macOS and iOS (iPhone/iPad). It allows the device to automatically start or stop an IKEv2 VPN connection based on various criteria. Refer to section 3.2 Configure IKEv2 VPN clients.

By default, the VPN On Demand rules created by the IKEv2 script automatically start a VPN connection when the device is on Wi-Fi (with captive portal detection), and stop the connection when it's on cellular. You can customize these rules to exclude certain Wi-Fi network(s) such as your home network, or to start the VPN connection both on Wi-Fi and cellular.

4.2 Customize VPN On Demand rules

To customize VPN On Demand rules for all new IKEv2 clients, edit **/opt/src/ikev2.sh** on your VPN server and replace the default rules with one of the examples below. After that, you may add new clients or re-export configurations for existing clients by running "sudo ikev2.sh".

To customize those rules for a specific IKEv2 client, edit the generated **.mobileconfig** file for that client. After that, remove the existing profile (if any) from the VPN client device and import the updated profile.

For reference, here are the default rules in the IKEv2 script:

```
<key>OnDemandRules</key>
<array>
  <dict>
    <key>InterfaceTypeMatch</key>
    <string>WiFi</string>
    <key>URLStringProbe</key>
```

```
    <string>http://captive.apple.com/hotspot-detect.html</string>
    <key>Action</key>
    <string>Connect</string>
  </dict>
  <dict>
    <key>InterfaceTypeMatch</key>
    <string>Cellular</string>
    <key>Action</key>
    <string>Disconnect</string>
  </dict>
  <dict>
    <key>Action</key>
    <string>Ignore</string>
  </dict>
</array>
```

Example 1: Exclude certain Wi-Fi network(s) from VPN On Demand:

```
<key>OnDemandRules</key>
<array>
  <dict>
    <key>InterfaceTypeMatch</key>
    <string>WiFi</string>
    <key>SSIDMatch</key>
    <array>
      <string>YOUR_WIFI_NETWORK_NAME</string>
    </array>
    <key>Action</key>
    <string>Disconnect</string>
  </dict>
  <dict>
    <key>InterfaceTypeMatch</key>
    <string>WiFi</string>
    <key>URLStringProbe</key>
    <string>http://captive.apple.com/hotspot-detect.html</string>
    <key>Action</key>
    <string>Connect</string>
  </dict>
```

```
<dict>
  <key>InterfaceTypeMatch</key>
  <string>Cellular</string>
  <key>Action</key>
  <string>Disconnect</string>
</dict>
<dict>
  <key>Action</key>
  <string>Ignore</string>
</dict>
</array>
```

Compared to the default rules, this part has been added in this example:

```
... ...
  <dict>
    <key>InterfaceTypeMatch</key>
    <string>WiFi</string>
    <key>SSIDMatch</key>
    <array>
      <string>YOUR_WIFI_NETWORK_NAME</string>
    </array>
    <key>Action</key>
    <string>Disconnect</string>
  </dict>
... ...
```

Note: If you have more than one Wi-Fi network to exclude, add more lines to the "SSIDMatch" section above. For example:

```
<array>
  <string>YOUR_WIFI_NETWORK_NAME_1</string>
  <string>YOUR_WIFI_NETWORK_NAME_2</string>
</array>
```

Example 2: Start the VPN connection also on cellular, in addition to Wi-Fi:

```
<key>OnDemandRules</key>
<array>
```

```
<dict>
    <key>InterfaceTypeMatch</key>
    <string>WiFi</string>
    <key>URLStringProbe</key>
    <string>http://captive.apple.com/hotspot-detect.html</string>
    <key>Action</key>
    <string>Connect</string>
</dict>
<dict>
    <key>InterfaceTypeMatch</key>
    <string>Cellular</string>
    <key>Action</key>
    <string>Connect</string>
</dict>
<dict>
    <key>Action</key>
    <string>Ignore</string>
</dict>
</array>
```

Compared to the default rules, this part has changed in this example:

```
... ...
    <dict>
        <key>InterfaceTypeMatch</key>
        <string>Cellular</string>
        <key>Action</key>
        <string>Connect</string>
    </dict>
... ...
```

Learn more about VPN On Demand rules in the Apple documentation (https://developer.apple.com/documentation/devicemanagement/vpn/vpn/ondemandruleselement).

5 Configure IPsec/L2TP VPN Clients

After setting up your own VPN server, follow these steps to configure your devices. IPsec/L2TP is natively supported by Android, iOS, OS X, and Windows. There is no additional software to install. Setup should only take a few minutes. In case you are unable to connect, first check to make sure the VPN credentials were entered correctly.

- Platforms
  - Windows
  - OS X (macOS)
  - Android
  - iOS (iPhone/iPad)
  - Chrome OS (Chromebook)
  - Linux

5.1 Windows

> You may also connect using **IKEv2** mode (recommended).

5.1.1 Windows 11

1. Right-click on the wireless/network icon in your system tray.
2. Select **Network and Internet settings**, then on the page that opens, click **VPN**.
3. Click the **Add VPN** button.
4. Select **Windows (built-in)** in the **VPN provider** drop-down menu.
5. Enter anything you like in the **Connection name** field.
6. Enter `Your VPN Server IP` in the **Server name or address** field.
7. Select **L2TP/IPsec with pre-shared key** in the **VPN type** drop-down menu.
8. Enter `Your VPN IPsec PSK` in the **Pre-shared key** field.
9. Enter `Your VPN Username` in the **User name** field.
10. Enter `Your VPN Password` in the **Password** field.

11. Check the **Remember my sign-in info** checkbox.
12. Click **Save** to save the VPN connection details.

Note: This one-time registry change (see section 7.3.1) is required if the VPN server and/or client is behind NAT (e.g. home router).

To connect to the VPN: Click the **Connect** button, or click on the wireless/network icon in your system tray, click **VPN**, then select the new VPN entry and click **Connect**. If prompted, enter `Your VPN Username` and `Password`, then click **OK**. You can verify that your traffic is being routed properly by looking up your IP address on Google. It should say "Your public IP address is `Your VPN Server IP`".

If you get an error when trying to connect, see section 7.3 IKEv1 troubleshooting.

5.1.2 Windows 10 and 8

1. Right-click on the wireless/network icon in your system tray.
2. Select **Open Network & Internet settings**, then on the page that opens, click **Network and Sharing Center**.
3. Click **Set up a new connection or network**.
4. Select **Connect to a workplace** and click **Next**.
5. Click **Use my Internet connection (VPN)**.
6. Enter `Your VPN Server IP` in the **Internet address** field.
7. Enter anything you like in the **Destination name** field, and then click **Create**.
8. Return to **Network and Sharing Center**. On the left, click **Change adapter settings**.
9. Right-click on the new VPN entry and choose **Properties**.
10. Click the **Security** tab. Select "Layer 2 Tunneling Protocol with IPsec (L2TP/IPSec)" for the **Type of VPN**.
11. Click **Allow these protocols**. Check the "Challenge Handshake Authentication Protocol (CHAP)" and "Microsoft CHAP Version 2 (MS-CHAP v2)" checkboxes.
12. Click the **Advanced settings** button.
13. Select **Use preshared key for authentication** and enter `Your VPN IPsec PSK` for the **Key**.

14. Click **OK** to close the **Advanced settings**.
15. Click **OK** to save the VPN connection details.

Note: This one-time registry change (see section 7.3.1) is required if the VPN server and/or client is behind NAT (e.g. home router).

To connect to the VPN: Click on the wireless/network icon in your system tray, select the new VPN entry, and click **Connect**. If prompted, enter Your VPN Username and Password, then click **OK**. You can verify that your traffic is being routed properly by looking up your IP address on Google. It should say "Your public IP address is Your VPN Server IP".

If you get an error when trying to connect, see section 7.3 IKEv1 troubleshooting.

Alternatively, instead of following the steps above, you may create the VPN connection using these Windows PowerShell commands. Replace Your VPN Server IP and Your VPN IPsec PSK with your own values, enclosed in single quotes:

```
# Disable persistent command history
Set-PSReadlineOption -HistorySaveStyle SaveNothing
# Create VPN connection
Add-VpnConnection -Name 'My IPsec VPN' `
  -ServerAddress 'Your VPN Server IP' `
  -L2tpPsk 'Your VPN IPsec PSK' -TunnelType L2tp `
  -EncryptionLevel Required `
  -AuthenticationMethod Chap,MSChapv2 -Force `
  -RememberCredential -PassThru
# Ignore the data encryption warning (data is encrypted
# in the IPsec tunnel)
```

5.1.3 Windows 7, Vista and XP

1. Click on the Start Menu and go to the Control Panel.
2. Go to the **Network and Internet** section.
3. Click **Network and Sharing Center**.
4. Click **Set up a new connection or network**.
5. Select **Connect to a workplace** and click **Next**.

6. Click **Use my Internet connection (VPN)**.

7. Enter Your VPN Server IP in the **Internet address** field.

8. Enter anything you like in the **Destination name** field.

9. Check the **Don't connect now; just set it up so I can connect later** checkbox.

10. Click **Next**.

11. Enter Your VPN Username in the **User name** field.

12. Enter Your VPN Password in the **Password** field.

13. Check the **Remember this password** checkbox.

14. Click **Create**, and then **Close**.

15. Return to **Network and Sharing Center**. On the left, click **Change adapter settings**.

16. Right-click on the new VPN entry and choose **Properties**.

17. Click the **Options** tab and uncheck **Include Windows logon domain**.

18. Click the **Security** tab. Select "Layer 2 Tunneling Protocol with IPsec (L2TP/IPSec)" for the **Type of VPN**.

19. Click **Allow these protocols**. Check the "Challenge Handshake Authentication Protocol (CHAP)" and "Microsoft CHAP Version 2 (MS-CHAP v2)" checkboxes.

20. Click the **Advanced settings** button.

21. Select **Use preshared key for authentication** and enter Your VPN IPsec PSK for the **Key**.

22. Click **OK** to close the **Advanced settings**.

23. Click **OK** to save the VPN connection details.

Note: This one-time registry change (see section 7.3.1) is required if the VPN server and/or client is behind NAT (e.g. home router).

To connect to the VPN: Click on the wireless/network icon in your system tray, select the new VPN entry, and click **Connect**. If prompted, enter Your VPN Username and Password, then click **OK**. You can verify that your traffic is being routed properly by looking up your IP address on Google. It should say "Your public IP address is Your VPN Server IP".

If you get an error when trying to connect, see section 7.3 IKEv1 troubleshooting.

5.2 OS X (macOS)

5.2.1 macOS 13 (Ventura) and newer

> You may also connect using IKEv2 (recommended) or IPsec/XAuth mode.

1. Open **System Settings** and go to the **Network** section.
2. Click **VPN** on the right hand side of the window.
3. Click the **Add VPN Configuration** drop-down menu and select **L2TP over IPSec**.
4. In the window that opens, enter anything you like for the **Display name**.
5. Leave **Configuration** as **Default**.
6. Enter `Your VPN Server IP` for the **Server address**.
7. Enter `Your VPN Username` for the **Account name**.
8. Select **Password** from the **User authentication** drop-down menu.
9. Enter `Your VPN Password` for the **Password**.
10. Select **Shared secret** from the **Machine authentication** drop-down menu.
11. Enter `Your VPN IPsec PSK` for the **Shared secret**.
12. Leave the **Group name** field blank.
13. **(Important)** Click the **Options** tab, and make sure the **Send all traffic over VPN connection** toggle is ON.
14. **(Important)** Click the **TCP/IP** tab, and select **Link-local only** from the **Configure IPv6** drop-down menu.
15. Click **Create** to save the VPN configuration.
16. To show VPN status in your menu bar and for shortcut access, go to the **Control Center** section of **System Settings**. Scroll to the bottom and select `Show in Menu Bar` from the **VPN** drop-down menu.

To connect to the VPN: Use the menu bar icon, or go to the **VPN** section of **System Settings** and toggle the switch for your VPN configuration. You can verify that your traffic is being routed properly by looking up your IP address on Google. It should say "Your public IP address is `Your VPN Server IP`".

If you get an error when trying to connect, see section 7.3 IKEv1 troubleshooting.

5.2.2 macOS 12 (Monterey) and older

> You may also connect using IKEv2 (recommended) or IPsec/XAuth
> mode.

1. Open System Preferences and go to the Network section.
2. Click the + button in the lower-left corner of the window.
3. Select **VPN** from the **Interface** drop-down menu.
4. Select **L2TP over IPSec** from the **VPN Type** drop-down menu.
5. Enter anything you like for the **Service Name**.
6. Click **Create**.
7. Enter Your VPN Server IP for the **Server Address**.
8. Enter Your VPN Username for the **Account Name**.
9. Click the **Authentication Settings** button.
10. In the **User Authentication** section, select the **Password** radio button and enter Your VPN Password.
11. In the **Machine Authentication** section, select the **Shared Secret** radio button and enter Your VPN IPsec PSK.
12. Click **OK**.
13. Check the **Show VPN status in menu bar** checkbox.
14. **(Important)** Click the **Advanced** button and make sure the **Send all traffic over VPN connection** checkbox is checked.
15. **(Important)** Click the **TCP/IP** tab, and make sure **Link-local only** is selected in the **Configure IPv6** section.
16. Click **OK** to close the Advanced settings, and then click **Apply** to save the VPN connection information.

To connect to the VPN: Use the menu bar icon, or go to the Network section of System Preferences, select the VPN and choose **Connect**. You can verify that your traffic is being routed properly by looking up your IP address on Google. It should say "Your public IP address is Your VPN Server IP".

If you get an error when trying to connect, see section 7.3 IKEv1 troubleshooting.

5.3 Android

Important: Android users should instead connect using IKEv2 mode (recommended), which is more secure. See section 3.2 for more details. Android 12+ only supports IKEv2 mode. The native VPN client in Android uses the less secure `modp1024` (DH group 2) for the IPsec/L2TP and IPsec/XAuth ("Cisco IPsec") modes.

If you still want to connect using IPsec/L2TP mode, you must first edit `/etc/ipsec.conf` on the VPN server. Find the line `ike=...` and append `,aes256-sha2;modp1024,aes128-sha1;modp1024` at the end. Save the file and run `sudo service ipsec restart`.

Docker users: Add `VPN_ENABLE_MODP1024=yes` to your env file, then re-create the Docker container.

After that, follow the steps below on your Android device:

1. Launch the **Settings** application.
2. Tap "Network & internet". Or, if using Android 7 or earlier, tap **More...** in the **Wireless & networks** section.
3. Tap **VPN**.
4. Tap **Add VPN Profile** or the + icon at top-right of screen.
5. Enter anything you like in the **Name** field.
6. Select **L2TP/IPSec PSK** in the **Type** drop-down menu.
7. Enter `Your VPN Server IP` in the **Server address** field.
8. Leave the **L2TP secret** field blank.
9. Leave the **IPSec identifier** field blank.
10. Enter `Your VPN IPsec PSK` in the **IPSec pre-shared key** field.
11. Tap **Save**.
12. Tap the new VPN connection.
13. Enter `Your VPN Username` in the **Username** field.
14. Enter `Your VPN Password` in the **Password** field.
15. Check the **Save account information** checkbox.
16. Tap **Connect**.

Once connected, you will see a VPN icon in the notification bar. You can verify that your traffic is being routed properly by looking up your IP address on Google. It should say "Your public IP address is `Your VPN Server IP`".

If you get an error when trying to connect, see section 7.3 IKEv1 troubleshooting.

5.4 iOS

> You may also connect using IKEv2 (recommended) or IPsec/XAuth mode.

1. Go to Settings -> General -> VPN.
2. Tap **Add VPN Configuration...**.
3. Tap **Type**. Select **L2TP** and go back.
4. Tap **Description** and enter anything you like.
5. Tap **Server** and enter Your VPN Server IP.
6. Tap **Account** and enter Your VPN Username.
7. Tap **Password** and enter Your VPN Password.
8. Tap **Secret** and enter Your VPN IPsec PSK.
9. Make sure the **Send All Traffic** switch is ON.
10. Tap **Done**.
11. Slide the **VPN** switch ON.

Once connected, you will see a VPN icon in the status bar. You can verify that your traffic is being routed properly by looking up your IP address on Google. It should say "Your public IP address is Your VPN Server IP".

If you get an error when trying to connect, see section 7.3 IKEv1 troubleshooting.

5.5 Chrome OS

> You may also connect using IKEv2 mode (recommended).

1. Go to Settings -> Network.
2. Click **Add connection**, then click **Add built-in VPN**.
3. Enter anything you like for the **Service name**.
4. Select **L2TP/IPsec** in the **Provider type** drop-down menu.
5. Enter Your VPN Server IP for the **Server hostname**.
6. Select **Pre-shared key** in the **Authentication type** drop-down menu.

7. Enter `Your VPN Username` for the **Username**.
8. Enter `Your VPN Password` for the **Password**.
9. Enter `Your VPN IPsec PSK` for the **Pre-shared key**.
10. Leave other fields blank.
11. Enable **Save identity and password**.
12. Click **Connect**.

Once connected, you will see a VPN icon overlay on the network status icon. You can verify that your traffic is being routed properly by looking up your IP address on Google. It should say "Your public IP address is `Your VPN Server IP`".

If you get an error when trying to connect, see section 7.3 IKEv1 troubleshooting.

5.6 Linux

> You may also connect using IKEv2 mode (recommended).

5.6.1 Ubuntu Linux

Ubuntu 18.04 (and newer) users can install the network-manager-l2tp-gnome package using `apt`, then configure the IPsec/L2TP VPN client using the GUI.

1. Go to Settings -> Network -> VPN. Click the + button.
2. Select **Layer 2 Tunneling Protocol (L2TP)**.
3. Enter anything you like in the **Name** field.
4. Enter `Your VPN Server IP` for the **Gateway**.
5. Enter `Your VPN Username` for the **User name**.
6. Right-click the **?** in the **Password** field, select **Store the password only for this user**.
7. Enter `Your VPN Password` for the **Password**.
8. Leave the **NT Domain** field blank.
9. Click the **IPsec Settings...** button.
10. Check the **Enable IPsec tunnel to L2TP host** checkbox.
11. Leave the **Gateway ID** field blank.
12. Enter `Your VPN IPsec PSK` for the **Pre-shared key**.

13. Expand the **Advanced** section.
14. Enter `aes128-sha1-modp2048` for the **Phase1 Algorithms**.
15. Enter `aes128-sha1` for the **Phase2 Algorithms**.
16. Click **OK**, then click **Add** to save the VPN connection information.
17. Turn the **VPN** switch ON.

Once connected, you can verify that your traffic is being routed properly by looking up your IP address on Google. It should say "Your public IP address is `Your VPN Server IP`".

5.6.2 Fedora and CentOS

Fedora 28 (and newer) and CentOS 8/7 users can connect using IPsec/XAuth mode.

5.6.3 Other Linux

First check here (https://github.com/nm-l2tp/NetworkManager-l2tp/wiki/Prebuilt-Packages) to see if the `network-manager-l2tp` and `network-manager-l2tp-gnome` packages are available for your Linux distribution. If yes, install them (select strongSwan) and follow the instructions above. Alternatively, you may configure Linux VPN clients using the command line.

5.6.4 Configure using the command line

Advanced users can follow these steps to configure Linux VPN clients using the command line. Alternatively, you may connect using IKEv2 mode (recommended), or configure using the GUI. Commands must be run as `root` on your VPN client.

To set up the VPN client, first install the following packages:

```
# Ubuntu and Debian
apt-get update
apt-get install strongswan xl2tpd net-tools


# Fedora
```

```
yum install strongswan xl2tpd net-tools

# CentOS
yum install epel-release
yum --enablerepo=epel install strongswan xl2tpd net-tools
```

Create VPN variables (replace with actual values):

```
VPN_SERVER_IP='your_vpn_server_ip'
VPN_IPSEC_PSK='your_ipsec_pre_shared_key'
VPN_USER='your_vpn_username'
VPN_PASSWORD='your_vpn_password'
```

Configure strongSwan:

```
cat > /etc/ipsec.conf <<EOF
# ipsec.conf - strongSwan IPsec configuration file

conn myvpn
  auto=add
  keyexchange=ikev1
  authby=secret
  type=transport
  left=%defaultroute
  leftprotoport=17/1701
  rightprotoport=17/1701
  right=$VPN_SERVER_IP
  ike=aes128-sha1-modp2048
  esp=aes128-sha1
EOF

cat > /etc/ipsec.secrets <<EOF
: PSK "$VPN_IPSEC_PSK"
EOF

chmod 600 /etc/ipsec.secrets

# For CentOS and Fedora ONLY
mv /etc/strongswan/ipsec.conf \
```

```
  /etc/strongswan/ipsec.conf.old 2>/dev/null
mv /etc/strongswan/ipsec.secrets \
  /etc/strongswan/ipsec.secrets.old 2>/dev/null
ln -s /etc/ipsec.conf /etc/strongswan/ipsec.conf
ln -s /etc/ipsec.secrets /etc/strongswan/ipsec.secrets
```

Configure xl2tpd:

```
cat > /etc/xl2tpd/xl2tpd.conf <<EOF
[lac myvpn]
lns = $VPN_SERVER_IP
ppp debug = yes
pppoptfile = /etc/ppp/options.l2tpd.client
length bit = yes
EOF


cat > /etc/ppp/options.l2tpd.client <<EOF
ipcp-accept-local
ipcp-accept-remote
refuse-eap
require-chap
noccp
noauth
mtu 1280
mru 1280
noipdefault
defaultroute
usepeerdns
connect-delay 5000
name "$VPN_USER"
password "$VPN_PASSWORD"
EOF


chmod 600 /etc/ppp/options.l2tpd.client
```

The VPN client setup is now complete. Follow the steps below to connect.

Note: You must repeat all steps below every time you try to connect to the VPN.

Create xl2tpd control file:

```
mkdir -p /var/run/xl2tpd
touch /var/run/xl2tpd/l2tp-control
```

Restart services:

```
service strongswan restart

# For Ubuntu 20.04, if strongswan service not found
ipsec restart

service xl2tpd restart
```

Start the IPsec connection:

```
# Ubuntu and Debian
ipsec up myvpn

# CentOS and Fedora
strongswan up myvpn
```

Start the L2TP connection:

```
echo "c myvpn" > /var/run/xl2tpd/l2tp-control
```

Run `ifconfig` and check the output. You should now see a new interface `ppp0`.

Check your existing default route:

```
ip route
```

Find this line in the output: `default via X.X.X.X ....` Write down this gateway IP for use in the two commands below.

Exclude your VPN server's public IP from the new default route (replace with actual value):

```
route add YOUR_VPN_SERVER_PUBLIC_IP gw X.X.X.X
```

If your VPN client is a remote server, you must also exclude your Local PC's public IP from the new default route, to prevent your SSH session from being disconnected (replace with actual value):

```
route add YOUR_LOCAL_PC_PUBLIC_IP gw X.X.X.X
```

Add a new default route to start routing traffic via the VPN server:

```
route add default dev ppp0
```

The VPN connection is now complete. Verify that your traffic is being routed properly:

```
wget -qO- http://ipv4.icanhazip.com; echo
```

The above command should return Your VPN Server IP.

To stop routing traffic via the VPN server:

```
route del default dev ppp0
```

To disconnect:

```
# Ubuntu and Debian
echo "d myvpn" > /var/run/xl2tpd/l2tp-control
ipsec down myvpn

# CentOS and Fedora
echo "d myvpn" > /var/run/xl2tpd/l2tp-control
strongswan down myvpn
```

6   Configure   IPsec/XAuth   VPN Clients

After setting up your own VPN server, follow these steps to configure your devices. IPsec/XAuth ("Cisco IPsec") is natively supported by Android, iOS and OS X. There is no additional software to install. Windows users can use the free Shrew Soft client. In case you are unable to connect, first check to make sure the VPN credentials were entered correctly.

IPsec/XAuth mode is also called "Cisco IPsec". This mode is generally **faster than** IPsec/L2TP with less overhead.

- Platforms
    - Windows
    - OS X (macOS)
    - Android
    - iOS (iPhone/iPad)
    - Linux

6.1 Windows

> You may also connect using **IKEv2** (recommended) or **IPsec/L2TP** mode. No additional software is required.

1. Download and install the free Shrew Soft VPN client (https://www.shrew.net/download/vpn). When prompted during install, select **Standard Edition**.
   Note: This VPN client does NOT support Windows 10/11.
2. Click Start Menu -> All Programs -> ShrewSoft VPN Client -> VPN Access Manager
3. Click the **Add (+)** button on toolbar.
4. Enter `Your VPN Server IP` in the **Host Name or IP Address** field.
5. Click the **Authentication** tab. Select **Mutual PSK + XAuth** from the **Authentication Method** drop-down menu.

6. Under the **Local Identity** sub-tab, select **IP Address** from the **Identification Type** drop-down menu.

7. Click the **Credentials** sub-tab. Enter `Your VPN IPsec PSK` in the **Pre Shared Key** field.

8. Click the **Phase 1** tab. Select **main** from the **Exchange Type** drop-down menu.

9. Click the **Phase 2** tab. Select **sha1** from the **HMAC Algorithm** drop-down menu.

10. Click **Save** to save the VPN connection details.

11. Select the new VPN connection. Click the **Connect** button on toolbar.

12. Enter `Your VPN Username` in the **Username** field.

13. Enter `Your VPN Password` in the **Password** field.

14. Click **Connect**.

Once connected, you will see **tunnel enabled** in the VPN Connect status window. Click the "Network" tab, and confirm that **Established - 1** is displayed under "Security Associations". You can verify that your traffic is being routed properly by looking up your IP address on Google. It should say "Your public IP address is `Your VPN Server IP`".

If you get an error when trying to connect, see section 7.3 IKEv1 troubleshooting.

6.2 OS X (macOS)

6.2.1 macOS 13 (Ventura) and newer

> You may also connect using IKEv2 (recommended) or IPsec/L2TP mode.

1. Open **System Settings** and go to the **Network** section.

2. Click **VPN** on the right hand side of the window.

3. Click the **Add VPN Configuration** drop-down menu and select **Cisco IPSec**.

4. In the window that opens, enter anything you like for the **Display name**.

5. Enter `Your VPN Server IP` for the **Server address**.

6. Enter Your VPN Username for the **Account name**.

7. Enter Your VPN Password for the **Password**.

8. Select **Shared secret** from the **Type** drop-down menu.

9. Enter Your VPN IPsec PSK for the **Shared secret**.

10. Leave the **Group name** field blank.

11. Click **Create** to save the VPN configuration.

12. To show VPN status in your menu bar and for shortcut access, go to the **Control Center** section of **System Settings**. Scroll to the bottom and select Show in Menu Bar from the **VPN** drop-down menu.

To connect to the VPN: Use the menu bar icon, or go to the **VPN** section of **System Settings** and toggle the switch for your VPN configuration. You can verify that your traffic is being routed properly by looking up your IP address on Google. It should say "Your public IP address is Your VPN Server IP".

If you get an error when trying to connect, see section 7.3 IKEv1 troubleshooting.

6.2.2 macOS 12 (Monterey) and older

> You may also connect using IKEv2 (recommended) or IPsec/L2TP mode.

1. Open System Preferences and go to the Network section.

2. Click the + button in the lower-left corner of the window.

3. Select **VPN** from the **Interface** drop-down menu.

4. Select **Cisco IPSec** from the **VPN Type** drop-down menu.

5. Enter anything you like for the **Service Name**.

6. Click **Create**.

7. Enter Your VPN Server IP for the **Server Address**.

8. Enter Your VPN Username for the **Account Name**.

9. Enter Your VPN Password for the **Password**.

10. Click the **Authentication Settings** button.

11. In the **Machine Authentication** section, select the **Shared Secret** radio button and enter Your VPN IPsec PSK.

12. Leave the **Group Name** field blank.

13. Click **OK**.

14. Check the **Show VPN status in menu bar** checkbox.

15. Click **Apply** to save the VPN connection information.

To connect to the VPN: Use the menu bar icon, or go to the Network section of System Preferences, select the VPN and choose **Connect**. You can verify that your traffic is being routed properly by looking up your IP address on Google. It should say "Your public IP address is `Your VPN Server IP`".

If you get an error when trying to connect, see section 7.3 IKEv1 troubleshooting.

6.3 Android

Important: Android users should instead connect using IKEv2 mode (recommended), which is more secure. See section 3.2 for more details. Android 12+ only supports IKEv2 mode. The native VPN client in Android uses the less secure `modp1024` (DH group 2) for the IPsec/L2TP and IPsec/XAuth ("Cisco IPsec") modes.

If you still want to connect using IPsec/XAuth mode, you must first edit `/etc/ipsec.conf` on the VPN server. Find the line `ike=...` and append `,aes256-sha2;modp1024,aes128-sha1;modp1024` at the end. Save the file and run `sudo service ipsec restart`.

Docker users: Add `VPN_ENABLE_MODP1024=yes` to your env file, then re-create the Docker container.

After that, follow the steps below on your Android device:

1. Launch the **Settings** application.
2. Tap "Network & internet". Or, if using Android 7 or earlier, tap **More...** in the **Wireless & networks** section.
3. Tap **VPN**.
4. Tap **Add VPN Profile** or the + icon at top-right of screen.
5. Enter anything you like in the **Name** field.
6. Select **IPSec Xauth PSK** in the **Type** drop-down menu.
7. Enter `Your VPN Server IP` in the **Server address** field.
8. Leave the **IPSec identifier** field blank.
9. Enter `Your VPN IPsec PSK` in the **IPSec pre-shared key** field.
10. Tap **Save**.

11. Tap the new VPN connection.

12. Enter `Your VPN Username` in the **Username** field.

13. Enter `Your VPN Password` in the **Password** field.

14. Check the **Save account information** checkbox.

15. Tap **Connect**.

Once connected, you will see a VPN icon in the notification bar. You can verify that your traffic is being routed properly by looking up your IP address on Google. It should say "Your public IP address is `Your VPN Server IP`".

If you get an error when trying to connect, see section 7.3 IKEv1 troubleshooting.

6.4 iOS

> You may also connect using IKEv2 (recommended) or IPsec/L2TP mode.

1. Go to Settings -> General -> VPN.

2. Tap **Add VPN Configuration...**.

3. Tap **Type**. Select **IPSec** and go back.

4. Tap **Description** and enter anything you like.

5. Tap **Server** and enter `Your VPN Server IP`.

6. Tap **Account** and enter `Your VPN Username`.

7. Tap **Password** and enter `Your VPN Password`.

8. Leave the **Group Name** field blank.

9. Tap **Secret** and enter `Your VPN IPsec PSK`.

10. Tap **Done**.

11. Slide the **VPN** switch ON.

Once connected, you will see a VPN icon in the status bar. You can verify that your traffic is being routed properly by looking up your IP address on Google. It should say "Your public IP address is `Your VPN Server IP`".

If you get an error when trying to connect, see section 7.3 IKEv1 troubleshooting.

6.5 Linux

> You may also connect using IKEv2 mode (recommended).

6.5.1 Fedora and CentOS

Fedora 28 (and newer) and CentOS 8/7 users can install the `NetworkManager-libreswan-gnome` package using yum, then configure the IPsec/XAuth VPN client using the GUI.

1. Go to Settings -> Network -> VPN. Click the + button.
2. Select **IPsec based VPN**.
3. Enter anything you like in the **Name** field.
4. Enter `Your VPN Server IP` for the **Gateway**.
5. Select **IKEv1 (XAUTH)** in the **Type** drop-down menu.
6. Enter `Your VPN Username` for the **User name**.
7. Right-click the **?** in the **User password** field, select **Store the password only for this user**.
8. Enter `Your VPN Password` for the **User password**.
9. Leave the **Group name** field blank.
10. Right-click the **?** in the **Secret** field, select **Store the password only for this user**.
11. Enter `Your VPN IPsec PSK` for the **Secret**.
12. Leave the **Remote ID** field blank.
13. Click **Add** to save the VPN connection information.
14. Turn the **VPN** switch ON.

Once connected, you can verify that your traffic is being routed properly by looking up your IP address on Google. It should say "Your public IP address is `Your VPN Server IP`".

6.5.2 Other Linux

Other Linux users can connect using IPsec/L2TP mode.

7 IPsec VPN: Troubleshooting

- Check logs and VPN status
- IKEv2 troubleshooting
  - Cannot connect to the VPN server
  - Unable to connect multiple IKEv2 clients
  - IKE authentication credentials are unacceptable
  - Policy match error
  - Parameter is incorrect
  - Cannot open websites after connecting to IKEv2
  - Windows 10 connecting
  - Other known issues
- IKEv1 troubleshooting
  - Windows error 809
  - Windows error 789 or 691
  - Windows error 628 or 766
  - Windows 10/11 upgrades
  - Windows DNS leaks and IPv6
  - Android/Linux MTU/MSS issues
  - macOS send traffic over VPN
  - iOS/Android sleep mode
  - Debian kernel

7.1 Check logs and VPN status

Commands below must be run as `root` (or using `sudo`).

First, restart services on the VPN server:

```
service ipsec restart
service xl2tpd restart
```

Docker users: Run `docker restart ipsec-vpn-server`.

Then reboot your VPN client device, and retry the connection. If still unable to connect, try removing and recreating the VPN connection. Make sure that the VPN server address and VPN credentials are entered correctly.

For servers with an external firewall (e.g. EC2/GCE), open UDP ports 500 and 4500 for the VPN.

Check the Libreswan (IPsec) and xl2tpd logs for errors:

```
# Ubuntu & Debian
grep pluto /var/log/auth.log
grep xl2tpd /var/log/syslog


# CentOS/RHEL, Rocky Linux, AlmaLinux,
# Oracle Linux & Amazon Linux 2
grep pluto /var/log/secure
grep xl2tpd /var/log/messages


# Alpine Linux
grep pluto /var/log/messages
grep xl2tpd /var/log/messages
```

Check the status of the IPsec VPN server:

```
ipsec status
```

Show currently established VPN connections:

```
ipsec trafficstatus
```

7.2 IKEv2 troubleshooting

See also: 7.1 Check logs and VPN status, 7.3 IKEv1 troubleshooting and chapter 8, IPsec VPN: Advanced Usage.

- Cannot connect to the VPN server
- Unable to connect multiple IKEv2 clients
- IKE authentication credentials are unacceptable
- Policy match error

- Parameter is incorrect
- Cannot open websites after connecting to IKEv2
- Windows 10 connecting
- Other known issues

7.2.1 Cannot connect to the VPN server

First, make sure that the VPN server address specified on your VPN client device **exactly matches** the server address in the output of the IKEv2 helper script. For example, you cannot use a DNS name to connect if it was not specified when setting up IKEv2. To change the IKEv2 server address, read section 3.4 Change IKEv2 server address.

For servers with an external firewall (e.g. EC2/GCE), open UDP ports 500 and 4500 for the VPN.

Check logs and VPN status for errors (see section 7.1). If you encounter retransmission related errors and are unable to connect, there may be network issues between the VPN client and server.

7.2.2 Unable to connect multiple IKEv2 clients

To connect multiple IKEv2 clients from behind the same NAT (e.g. home router) at the same time, you will need to generate a unique certificate for each client. Otherwise, you could encounter the issue where a later connected client affects the VPN connection of an existing client, which may lose Internet access.

To generate certificates for additional IKEv2 clients, run the helper script with the --addclient option. To customize client options, run the script without arguments.

```
sudo ikev2.sh --addclient [client name]
```

7.2.3 IKE authentication credentials are unacceptable

If you encounter this error, make sure that the VPN server address specified on your VPN client device **exactly matches** the server address in the output of the IKEv2 helper script. For example, you cannot use a DNS name to connect if it was not specified when setting up IKEv2. To change the IKEv2 server address, read section 3.4 Change IKEv2 server address.

7.2.4 Policy match error

To fix this error, you will need to enable stronger ciphers for IKEv2 with a one-time registry change. Run the following from an elevated command prompt.

- For Windows 7, 8, 10 and 11

```
REG ADD HKLM\SYSTEM\CurrentControlSet\Services\RasMan\Parameters ^
  /v NegotiateDH2048_AES256 /t REG_DWORD /d 0x1 /f
```

7.2.5 Parameter is incorrect

If you encounter "Error 87: The parameter is incorrect" when trying to connect using IKEv2 mode, try the solutions in: https://github.com/trailofbits/algo/issues/1051, more specifically, step 2 "reset device manager adapters".

7.2.6 Cannot open websites after connecting to IKEv2

If your VPN client device cannot open websites after successfully connecting to IKEv2, try the following fixes:

1. Some cloud providers, such as Google Cloud, set a lower MTU by default. This could cause network issues with IKEv2 VPN clients. To fix, try setting the MTU to 1500 on the VPN server:

   ```
   # Replace ens4 with the network interface name on your server
   sudo ifconfig ens4 mtu 1500
   ```

   This setting **does not** persist after a reboot. To change the MTU size permanently, refer to relevant articles on the web.

2. If your Android or Linux VPN client can connect using IKEv2 mode, but cannot open websites, try the fix in section 7.3.6 Android/Linux MTU/MSS issues.

3. Windows VPN clients may not use the DNS servers specified by IKEv2 after connecting, if the client's configured DNS servers on the Internet adapter are from the local network segment. This can be fixed by manually entering DNS servers such as Google Public DNS (8.8.8.8, 8.8.4.4) in network interface properties -> TCP/IPv4. For more information, see section 7.3.5 Windows DNS leaks and IPv6.

7.2.7 Windows 10 connecting

If using Windows 10 and the VPN is stuck on "connecting" for more than a few minutes, try these steps:

1. Right-click on the wireless/network icon in your system tray.
2. Select **Open Network & Internet settings**, then on the page that opens, click **VPN** on the left.
3. Select the new VPN entry, then click **Connect**.

7.2.8 Other known issues

The built-in VPN client in Windows may not support IKEv2 fragmentation (this feature requires Windows 10 v1803 or newer). On some networks, this can cause the connection to fail or have other issues. You may instead try the IPsec/L2TP or IPsec/XAuth mode.

7.3 IKEv1 troubleshooting

See also: 7.1 Check logs and VPN status, 7.2 IKEv2 troubleshooting and chapter 8, IPsec VPN: Advanced Usage.

- Windows error 809
- Windows error 789 or 691
- Windows error 628 or 766
- Windows 10/11 upgrades
- Windows DNS leaks and IPv6
- Android/Linux MTU/MSS issues
- macOS send traffic over VPN
- iOS/Android sleep mode

- Debian kernel

7.3.1 Windows error 809

> Error 809: The network connection between your computer and the VPN server could not be established because the remote server is not responding. This could be because one of the network devices (e.g, firewalls, NAT, routers, etc) between your computer and the remote server is not configured to allow VPN connections. Please contact your Administrator or your service provider to determine which device may be causing the problem.

Note: The registry change below is only required if you use IPsec/L2TP mode to connect to the VPN. It is NOT required for the IKEv2 and IPsec/XAuth modes.

To fix this error, a one-time registry change is required because the VPN server and/or client is behind NAT (e.g. home router). Run the following from an elevated command prompt. **You must reboot your PC when finished.**

- For Windows Vista, 7, 8, 10 and 11

```
REG ADD HKLM\SYSTEM\CurrentControlSet\Services\PolicyAgent ^
  /v AssumeUDPEncapsulationContextOnSendRule /t REG_DWORD ^
  /d 0x2 /f
```

- For Windows XP ONLY

```
REG ADD HKLM\SYSTEM\CurrentControlSet\Services\IPSec ^
  /v AssumeUDPEncapsulationContextOnSendRule /t REG_DWORD ^
  /d 0x2 /f
```

Although uncommon, some Windows systems disable IPsec encryption, causing the connection to fail. To re-enable it, run the following command and reboot your PC.

- For Windows XP, Vista, 7, 8, 10 and 11

```
REG ADD HKLM\SYSTEM\CurrentControlSet\Services\RasMan\Parameters ^
  /v ProhibitIpSec /t REG_DWORD /d 0x0 /f
```

7.3.2 Windows error 789 or 691

> Error 789: The L2TP connection attempt failed because the security layer encountered a processing error during initial negotiations with the remote computer.

> Error 691: The remote connection was denied because the user name and password combination you provided is not recognized, or the selected authentication protocol is not permitted on the remote access server.

For error 789, see: https://documentation.meraki.com/MX/Client_VPN/Troubleshooting_Client_VPN#Windows_Error_789 for troubleshooting information. For error 691, you may try removing and recreating the VPN connection. Make sure that the VPN credentials are entered correctly.

7.3.3 Windows error 628 or 766

> Error 628: The connection was terminated by the remote computer before it could be completed.

> Error 766: A certificate could not be found. Connections that use the L2TP protocol over IPSec require the installation of a machine certificate, also known as a computer certificate.

To fix these errors, please follow these steps:

1. Right-click on the wireless/network icon in your system tray.
2. Select **Open Network and Sharing Center**. Or, if using Windows 10 version 1709 or newer, select **Open Network & Internet settings**, then on the page that opens, click **Network and Sharing Center**.
3. On the left, click **Change adapter settings**. Right-click on the new VPN and choose **Properties**.
4. Click the **Security** tab. Select "Layer 2 Tunneling Protocol with IPsec (L2TP/IPSec)" for **Type of VPN**.

5. Click **Allow these protocols**. Check the "Challenge Handshake Authentication Protocol (CHAP)" and "Microsoft CHAP Version 2 (MS-CHAP v2)" checkboxes.
6. Click the **Advanced settings** button.
7. Select **Use preshared key for authentication** and enter Your VPN IPsec PSK for the **Key**.
8. Click **OK** to close the **Advanced settings**.
9. Click **OK** to save the VPN connection details.

7.3.4 Windows 10/11 upgrades

After upgrading Windows 10/11 version (e.g. from 21H2 to 22H2), you may need to re-apply the fix in section 7.3.1 for Windows Error 809 and reboot.

7.3.5 Windows DNS leaks and IPv6

Windows 8, 10 and 11 use "smart multi-homed name resolution" by default, which may cause "DNS leaks" when using the native IPsec VPN client if your DNS servers on the Internet adapter are from the local network segment. To fix, you may either disable smart multi-homed name resolution (https://www.neowin.net/news/guide-prevent-dns-leakage-while-using-a-vpn-on-windows-10-and-windows-8/), or configure your Internet adapter to use DNS servers outside your local network (e.g. 8.8.8.8 and 8.8.4.4). When finished, clear the DNS cache (https://support.opendns.com/hc/en-us/articles/227988627-How-to-clear-the-DNS-Cache-) and reboot your PC.

In addition, if your computer has IPv6 enabled, all IPv6 traffic (including DNS queries) will bypass the VPN. Learn how to disable IPv6 in Windows (https://support.microsoft.com/en-us/help/929852/guidance-for-configuring-ipv6-in-windows-for-advanced-users). If you need a VPN with IPv6 support, you could instead try OpenVPN. See chapter 13 for more details.

7.3.6 Android/Linux MTU/MSS issues

Some Android devices and Linux systems have MTU/MSS issues, that they are able to connect to the VPN using IPsec/XAuth ("Cisco IPsec") or IKEv2 mode, but cannot open websites. If you encounter this problem, try running the following commands on the VPN server. If successful, you may add these commands to /etc/rc.local to persist after reboot.

```
iptables -t mangle -A FORWARD -m policy --pol ipsec --dir in \
   -p tcp -m tcp --tcp-flags SYN,RST SYN -m tcpmss \
   --mss 1361:1536 -j TCPMSS --set-mss 1360
iptables -t mangle -A FORWARD -m policy --pol ipsec --dir out \
   -p tcp -m tcp --tcp-flags SYN,RST SYN -m tcpmss \
   --mss 1361:1536 -j TCPMSS --set-mss 1360


echo 1 > /proc/sys/net/ipv4/ip_no_pmtu_disc
```

Docker users: Instead of running the commands above, you may apply this fix by adding VPN_ANDROID_MTU_FIX=yes to your env file, then re-create the Docker container.

7.3.7 macOS send traffic over VPN

OS X (macOS) users: If you can successfully connect using IPsec/L2TP mode, but your public IP does not show Your VPN Server IP, read the OS X (macOS) section in chapter 5, Configure IPsec/L2TP VPN Clients, and complete these steps. Save VPN configuration and re-connect.

For macOS 13 (Ventura) and newer:

1. Click the **Options** tab, and make sure the **Send all traffic over VPN connection** toggle is ON.
2. Click the **TCP/IP** tab, and select **Link-local only** from the **Configure IPv6** drop-down menu.

For macOS 12 (Monterey) and older:

1. Click the **Advanced** button and make sure the **Send all traffic over VPN connection** checkbox is checked.
2. Click the **TCP/IP** tab, and make sure **Link-local only** is selected in the **Configure IPv6** section.

After trying the steps above, if your computer is still not sending traffic over the VPN, check the service order. From the main network preferences screen, select "set service order" in the cog drop down under the list of connections. Drag the VPN connection to the top.

7.3.8 iOS/Android sleep mode

To save battery, iOS devices (iPhone/iPad) will automatically disconnect Wi-Fi shortly after the screen turns off (sleep mode). As a result, the IPsec VPN disconnects. This behavior is by design and cannot be configured.

If you need the VPN to auto-reconnect when the device wakes up, you may connect using IKEv2 mode (recommended) and enable the "VPN On Demand" feature. Alternatively, you may try OpenVPN instead, which has support for options such as "Reconnect on Wakeup" and "Seamless Tunnel". See chapter 13 for more details.

Android devices may also disconnect Wi-Fi after entering sleep mode. You may try enabling the "Always-on VPN" option to stay connected. Learn more at:
https://support.google.com/android/answer/9089766

7.3.9 Debian kernel

Debian users: Run uname -r to check your server's Linux kernel version. If it contains the word "cloud", and /dev/ppp is missing, then the kernel lacks ppp support and cannot use IPsec/L2TP mode. The VPN setup scripts try to detect this and show a warning. In this case, you may instead use IKEv2 or IPsec/XAuth mode to connect to the VPN.

To fix the issue with IPsec/L2TP mode, you may switch to the standard Linux kernel by installing e.g. the linux-image-amd64 package. Then update the default kernel in GRUB and reboot your server.

8 IPsec VPN: Advanced Usage

- Use alternative DNS servers
- DNS name and server IP changes
- IKEv2-only VPN
- Internal VPN IPs and traffic
- Customize VPN subnets
- Port forwarding to VPN clients
- Split tunneling
- Access VPN server's subnet
- Access VPN clients from server's subnet
- Modify IPTables rules
- Deploy Google BBR congestion control

8.1 Use alternative DNS servers

Clients are set to use Google Public DNS: https://developers.google.com/speed/public-dns/ when the VPN is active. If another DNS provider is preferred, you may replace `8.8.8.8` and `8.8.4.4` in these files: `/etc/ppp/options.xl2tpd`, `/etc/ipsec.conf` and `/etc/ipsec.d/ikev2.conf` (if exists). Then run `service ipsec restart` and `service xl2tpd restart`.

Advanced users can define `VPN_DNS_SRV1` and optionally `VPN_DNS_SRV2` when running the VPN setup script and the IKEv2 helper script. For example, if you want to use Cloudflare's DNS service (https://1.1.1.1/dns/):

```
sudo VPN_DNS_SRV1=1.1.1.1 VPN_DNS_SRV2=1.0.0.1 sh vpn.sh
```

In certain circumstances, you may want VPN clients to use the specified DNS server(s) only for resolving internal domain name(s), and use their locally configured DNS servers to resolve all other domain names. This can be configured using the `modecfgdomains` option, e.g. `modecfgdomains="internal.example.com, home"`. Add this option to section conn ikev2-cp in `/etc/ipsec.d/ikev2.conf` for IKEv2, and to section conn xauth-psk in `/etc/ipsec.conf` for IPsec/XAuth ("Cisco IPsec"). Then run `service ipsec restart`. IPsec/L2TP mode does not support this option.

8.2 DNS name and server IP changes

For IPsec/L2TP and IPsec/XAuth ("Cisco IPsec") modes, you may use a DNS name (e.g. `vpn.example.com`) instead of an IP address to connect to the VPN server, without additional configuration. In addition, the VPN should generally continue to work after server IP changes, such as after restoring a snapshot to a new server with a different IP, although a reboot may be required.

For IKEv2 mode, if you want the VPN to continue to work after server IP changes, read section 3.4 Change IKEv2 server address. Alternatively, you may specify a DNS name for the IKEv2 server address when setting up IKEv2. The DNS name must be a fully qualified domain name (FQDN). Example:

```
sudo VPN_DNS_NAME='vpn.example.com' ikev2.sh --auto
```

Alternatively, you may customize IKEv2 options by running the helper script without the `--auto` parameter.

8.3 IKEv2-only VPN

Using Libreswan 4.2 or newer, advanced users can enable IKEv2-only mode on the VPN server. With IKEv2-only mode enabled, VPN clients can only connect to the VPN server using IKEv2. All IKEv1 connections (including IPsec/L2TP and IPsec/XAuth ("Cisco IPsec") modes) will be dropped.

To enable IKEv2-only mode, first install the VPN server and set up IKEv2. Then run the helper script and follow the prompts.

```
wget https://get.vpnsetup.net/ikev2only -O ikev2only.sh
sudo bash ikev2only.sh
```

To disable IKEv2-only mode, run the helper script again and select the appropriate option.

▼ Alternatively, you may manually enable IKEv2-only mode.

Alternatively, you may manually enable IKEv2-only mode. First check Libreswan version using `ipsec --version`, and update Libreswan (see section 2.7) if needed. Then edit `/etc/ipsec.conf` on the VPN server. Append `ikev1-policy=drop` to the end of the `config setup` section, indented by two spaces. Save the file and run `service ipsec restart`. When finished, you can run `ipsec status` to verify that only the `ikev2-cp` connection is enabled.

8.4 Internal VPN IPs and traffic

When connecting using IPsec/L2TP mode, the VPN server has internal IP `192.168.42.1` within the VPN subnet `192.168.42.0/24`. Clients are assigned internal IPs from `192.168.42.10` to `192.168.42.250`. To check which IP is assigned to a client, view the connection status on the VPN client.

When connecting using IPsec/XAuth ("Cisco IPsec") or IKEv2 mode, the VPN server does NOT have an internal IP within the VPN subnet `192.168.43.0/24`. Clients are assigned internal IPs from `192.168.43.10` to `192.168.43.250`.

You may use these internal VPN IPs for communication. However, note that the IPs assigned to VPN clients are dynamic, and firewalls on client devices may block such traffic.

Advanced users may optionally assign static IPs to VPN clients. See below for details.

▼ IPsec/L2TP mode: Assign static IPs to VPN clients.

The example below **ONLY** applies to IPsec/L2TP mode. Commands must be run as `root`.

1. First, create a new VPN user for each VPN client that you want to assign a static IP to. Refer to chapter 9, IPsec VPN: Manage VPN Users. Helper scripts are included for convenience.

2. Edit `/etc/xl2tpd/xl2tpd.conf` on the VPN server. Replace `ip range = 192.168.42.10-192.168.42.250` with e.g. `ip range = 192.168.42.100-192.168.42.250`. This reduces the pool of auto-assigned IP addresses, so that more IPs are available to assign to clients as static IPs.

3. Edit `/etc/ppp/chap-secrets` on the VPN server. For example, if the file contains:

```
"username1"  l2tpd  "password1"  *
"username2"  l2tpd  "password2"  *
"username3"  l2tpd  "password3"  *
```

Let's assume that you want to assign static IP `192.168.42.2` to VPN user `username2`, assign static IP `192.168.42.3` to VPN user `username3`, while keeping `username1` unchanged (auto-assign from the pool). After editing, the file should look like:

```
"username1"  l2tpd  "password1"  *
"username2"  l2tpd  "password2"  192.168.42.2
"username3"  l2tpd  "password3"  192.168.42.3
```

Note: The assigned static IP(s) must be from the subnet `192.168.42.0/24`, and must NOT be from the pool of auto-assigned IPs (see `ip range` above). In addition, `192.168.42.1` is reserved for the VPN server itself. In the example above, you can only assign static IP(s) from the range `192.168.42.2-192.168.42.99`.

4. **(Important)** Restart the xl2tpd service:

```
service xl2tpd restart
```

▼ IPsec/XAuth ("Cisco IPsec") mode: Assign static IPs to VPN clients.

The example below **ONLY** applies to IPsec/XAuth ("Cisco IPsec") mode. Commands must be run as `root`.

1. First, create a new VPN user for each VPN client that you want to assign a static IP to. Refer to chapter 9, IPsec VPN: Manage VPN Users. Helper scripts are included for convenience.

2. Edit `/etc/ipsec.conf` on the VPN server. Replace `rightaddresspool=192.168.43.10-192.168.43.250` with e.g. `rightaddresspool=192.168.43.100-192.168.43.250`. This reduces the pool of auto-assigned IP addresses, so that more IPs are available to assign to clients as static IPs.

3. Edit `/etc/ipsec.d/ikev2.conf` on the VPN server (if exists). Replace `rightaddresspool=192.168.43.10-192.168.43.250` with the **same value** as the previous step.

4. Edit `/etc/ipsec.d/passwd` on the VPN server. For example, if the file contains:

   ```
   username1:password1hashed:xauth-psk
   username2:password2hashed:xauth-psk
   username3:password3hashed:xauth-psk
   ```

   Let's assume that you want to assign static IP `192.168.43.2` to VPN user `username2`, assign static IP `192.168.43.3` to VPN user `username3`, while keeping `username1` unchanged (auto-assign from the pool). After editing, the file should look like:

   ```
   username1:password1hashed:xauth-psk
   username2:password2hashed:xauth-psk:192.168.42.2
   username3:password3hashed:xauth-psk:192.168.42.3
   ```

   Note: The assigned static IP(s) must be from the subnet `192.168.43.0/24`, and must NOT be from the pool of auto-assigned IPs (see `rightaddresspool` above). In the example above, you can only assign static IP(s) from the range `192.168.43.1-192.168.43.99`.

5. **(Important)** Restart the IPsec service:

   ```
   service ipsec restart
   ```

▼ IKEv2 mode: Assign static IPs to VPN clients.

The example below **ONLY** applies to IKEv2 mode. Commands must be run as `root`.

1. First, create a new IKEv2 client certificate for each client that you want to assign a static IP to, and write down the name of each IKEv2 client. Refer to section 3.3.1 Add a new IKEv2 client.

2. Edit `/etc/ipsec.d/ikev2.conf` on the VPN server. Replace `rightaddresspool=192.168.43.10–192.168.43.250` with e.g. `rightaddresspool=192.168.43.100–192.168.43.250`. This reduces the pool of auto-assigned IP addresses, so that more IPs are available to assign to clients as static IPs.

3. Edit `/etc/ipsec.conf` on the VPN server. Replace `rightaddresspool=192.168.43.10–192.168.43.250` with the **same value** as the previous step.

4. Edit `/etc/ipsec.d/ikev2.conf` on the VPN server again. For example, if the file contains:

```
conn ikev2-cp
  left=%defaultroute
  ... ...
```

Let's assume that you want to assign static IP `192.168.43.4` to IKEv2 client `client1`, assign static IP `192.168.43.5` to client `client2`, while keeping other clients unchanged (auto-assign from the pool). After editing, the file should look like:

```
conn ikev2-cp
  left=%defaultroute
  ... ...

conn client1
  rightid=@client1
  rightaddresspool=192.168.43.4–192.168.43.4
  also=ikev2-cp

conn client2
  rightid=@client2
```

```
rightaddresspool=192.168.43.5-192.168.43.5
also=ikev2-cp
```

Note: Add a new `conn` section for each client that you want to assign a static IP to. You must add a @ prefix to the client name for `rightid=`. The client name must exactly match the name you specified when adding the new IKEv2 client. The assigned static IP(s) must be from the subnet `192.168.43.0/24`, and must NOT be from the pool of auto-assigned IPs (see `rightaddresspool` above). In the example above, you can only assign static IP(s) from the range `192.168.43.1-192.168.43.99`.

Note: For Windows 7/8/10/11 clients, you must use a different syntax for `rightid=`. For example, if the client name is `client1`, set `rightid="CN=client1, O=IKEv2 VPN"` in the example above.

5. **(Important)** Restart the IPsec service:

```
service ipsec restart
```

Client-to-client traffic is allowed by default. If you want to **disallow** client-to-client traffic, run the following commands on the VPN server. Add them to /etc/rc.local to persist after reboot.

```
iptables -I FORWARD 2 -i ppp+ -o ppp+ -s 192.168.42.0/24 \
  -d 192.168.42.0/24 -j DROP
iptables -I FORWARD 3 -s 192.168.43.0/24 -d 192.168.43.0/24 \
  -j DROP
iptables -I FORWARD 4 -i ppp+ -d 192.168.43.0/24 -j DROP
iptables -I FORWARD 5 -s 192.168.43.0/24 -o ppp+ -j DROP
```

8.5 Customize VPN subnets

By default, IPsec/L2TP VPN clients will use internal VPN subnet `192.168.42.0/24`, while IPsec/XAuth ("Cisco IPsec") and IKEv2 VPN clients will use internal VPN subnet `192.168.43.0/24`. For more details, read the previous section.

For most use cases, it is NOT necessary and NOT recommended to customize these subnets. If your use case requires it, however, you may specify custom subnet(s) when installing the VPN.

Important: You may only specify custom subnets **during initial VPN install**. If the IPsec VPN is already installed, you **must** first uninstall the VPN (see chapter 10), then specify custom subnets and re-install. Otherwise, the VPN may stop working.

▼ First, read the important note above. Then view the examples.

```
# Example: Specify custom VPN subnet for IPsec/L2TP mode
# Note: All three variables must be specified.
sudo VPN_L2TP_NET=10.1.0.0/16 \
VPN_L2TP_LOCAL=10.1.0.1 \
VPN_L2TP_POOL=10.1.0.10-10.1.254.254 \
sh vpn.sh
```

```
# Example: Specify custom VPN subnet for IPsec/XAuth
#          and IKEv2 modes
# Note: Both variables must be specified.
sudo VPN_XAUTH_NET=10.2.0.0/16 \
VPN_XAUTH_POOL=10.2.0.10-10.2.254.254 \
sh vpn.sh
```

In the examples above, `VPN_L2TP_LOCAL` is the VPN server's internal IP for IPsec/L2TP mode. `VPN_L2TP_POOL` and `VPN_XAUTH_POOL` are the pools of auto-assigned IP addresses for VPN clients.

8.6 Port forwarding to VPN clients

In certain circumstances, you may want to forward port(s) on the VPN server to a connected VPN client. This can be done by adding IPTables rules on the VPN server.

Warning: Port forwarding will expose port(s) on the VPN client to the entire Internet, which could be a **security risk**! This is NOT recommended, unless your use case requires it.

Note: The internal VPN IPs assigned to VPN clients are dynamic, and firewalls on client devices may block forwarded traffic. To assign static IPs to VPN clients, refer to the previous section. To check which IP is assigned to a client, view the connection status on the VPN client.

Example 1: Forward TCP port 443 on the VPN server to the IPsec/L2TP client at 192.168.42.10.

```
# Get default network interface name
netif=$(ip -4 route list 0/0 | grep -m 1 -Po '(?<=dev )(\S+)')
iptables -I FORWARD 2 -i "$netif" -o ppp+ -p tcp --dport 443 \
  -j ACCEPT
iptables -t nat -A PREROUTING -p tcp --dport 443 \
  -j DNAT --to 192.168.42.10
```

Example 2: Forward UDP port 123 on the VPN server to the IKEv2 (or IPsec/XAuth) client at 192.168.43.10.

```
# Get default network interface name
netif=$(ip -4 route list 0/0 | grep -m 1 -Po '(?<=dev )(\S+)')
iptables -I FORWARD 2 -i "$netif" -d 192.168.43.0/24 \
  -p udp --dport 123 -j ACCEPT
iptables -t nat -A PREROUTING -p udp --dport 123 \
  -j DNAT --to 192.168.43.10
```

If you want the rules to persist after reboot, you may add these commands to /etc/rc.local. To remove the added IPTables rules, run the commands again, but replace -I FORWARD 2 with -D FORWARD, and replace -A PREROUTING with -D PREROUTING.

8.7 Split tunneling

With split tunneling, VPN clients will only send traffic for a specific destination subnet through the VPN tunnel. Other traffic will NOT go through the VPN tunnel. Split tunneling has some limitations, and is not supported by all VPN clients.

Advanced users can optionally enable split tunneling for the IPsec/XAuth ("Cisco IPsec") and/or IKEv2 modes. See below for details. IPsec/L2TP mode does NOT support this feature.

▼ IPsec/XAuth ("Cisco IPsec") mode: Enable split tunneling.

The example below **ONLY** applies to IPsec/XAuth ("Cisco IPsec") mode. Commands must be run as `root`.

1. Edit `/etc/ipsec.conf` on the VPN server. In the section `conn xauth-psk`, replace `leftsubnet=0.0.0.0/0` with the subnet you want VPN clients to send traffic through the VPN tunnel. For example:

   `leftsubnet=10.123.123.0/24`

2. **(Important)** Restart the IPsec service:

   `service ipsec restart`

▼ IKEv2 mode: Enable split tunneling.

The example below **ONLY** applies to IKEv2 mode. Commands must be run as `root`.

1. Edit `/etc/ipsec.d/ikev2.conf` on the VPN server. In the section `conn ikev2-cp`, replace `leftsubnet=0.0.0.0/0` with the subnet you want VPN clients to send traffic through the VPN tunnel. For example:

   `leftsubnet=10.123.123.0/24`

2. **(Important)** Restart the IPsec service:

   `service ipsec restart`

Note: Advanced users can set a different split tunneling configuration for specific IKEv2 client(s). Refer to "IKEv2 mode: Assign static IPs to VPN clients" in section 8.4 Internal VPN IPs and traffic. Based on the example provided in that section, you may add the `leftsubnet=...` option to the `conn` section of the specific IKEv2 client, then restart the IPsec service.

8.8 Access VPN server's subnet

After connecting to the VPN, VPN clients can generally access services running on other devices that are within the same local subnet as the VPN server, without additional configuration. For example, if the VPN server's local subnet is 192.168.0.0/24, and an Nginx server is running on IP 192.168.0.2, VPN clients can use IP 192.168.0.2 to access the Nginx server.

Please note, additional configuration is required if the VPN server has multiple network interfaces (e.g. eth0 and eth1), and you want VPN clients to access the local subnet behind the network interface that is NOT for Internet access. In this scenario, you must run the following commands to add IPTables rules. To persist after reboot, you may add these commands to /etc/rc.local.

```
# Replace eth1 with the name of the network interface
# on the VPN server that you want VPN clients to access
netif=eth1
iptables -I FORWARD 2 -i "$netif" -o ppp+ -m conntrack \
  --ctstate RELATED,ESTABLISHED -j ACCEPT
iptables -I FORWARD 2 -i ppp+ -o "$netif" -j ACCEPT
iptables -I FORWARD 2 -i "$netif" -d 192.168.43.0/24 \
  -m conntrack --ctstate RELATED,ESTABLISHED -j ACCEPT
iptables -I FORWARD 2 -s 192.168.43.0/24 -o "$netif" -j ACCEPT
iptables -t nat -I POSTROUTING -s 192.168.43.0/24 -o "$netif" \
  -m policy --dir out --pol none -j MASQUERADE
iptables -t nat -I POSTROUTING -s 192.168.42.0/24 -o "$netif" \
  -j MASQUERADE
```

8.9 Access VPN clients from server's subnet

In certain circumstances, you may need to access services on VPN clients from other devices that are on the same local subnet as the VPN server. This can be done using the following steps.

Assume that the VPN server IP is 10.1.0.2, and the IP of the device from which you want to access VPN clients is 10.1.0.3.

1. Add IPTables rules on the VPN server to allow this traffic. For example:

```
# Get default network interface name
netif=$(ip -4 route list 0/0 | grep -m 1 -Po '(?<=dev )(\S+)')
iptables -I FORWARD 2 -i "$netif" -o ppp+ -s 10.1.0.3 -j ACCEPT
iptables -I FORWARD 2 -i "$netif" -d 192.168.43.0/24 \
  -s 10.1.0.3 -j ACCEPT
```

2. Add routing rules on the device you want to access VPN clients. For example:

```
# Replace eth0 with the network interface name
# of the device's local subnet
route add -net 192.168.42.0 netmask 255.255.255.0 \
  gw 10.1.0.2 dev eth0
route add -net 192.168.43.0 netmask 255.255.255.0 \
  gw 10.1.0.2 dev eth0
```

Learn more about internal VPN IPs in section 8.4 Internal VPN IPs and traffic.

8.10 Modify IPTables rules

If you want to modify the IPTables rules after install, edit `/etc/iptables.rules` and/or `/etc/iptables/rules.v4` (Ubuntu/Debian), or `/etc/sysconfig/iptables` (CentOS/RHEL). Then reboot your server.

Note: If using Rocky Linux, AlmaLinux, Oracle Linux 8 or CentOS/RHEL 8 and firewalld was active during VPN setup, nftables may be configured. In this case, edit `/etc/sysconfig/nftables.conf` instead of `/etc/sysconfig/iptables`.

8.11 Deploy Google BBR congestion control

After the VPN server is set up, the performance can be improved by deploying the Google BBR congestion control algorithm.

This is usually done by modifying the configuration file `/etc/sysctl.conf`. However, some Linux distributions may additionally require updates to the Linux kernel.

For detailed deployment methods, please refer to:
https://github.com/hwdsl2/setup-ipsec-vpn/blob/master/docs/bbr.md

9 IPsec VPN: Manage VPN Users

By default, a single user account for VPN login is created. If you wish to view or manage users for the IPsec/L2TP and IPsec/XAuth ("Cisco IPsec") modes, read this chapter. For IKEv2, see section 3.3 Manage IKEv2 clients.

- Manage VPN users using helper scripts
- View VPN users
- View or update the IPsec PSK
- Manually manage VPN users

9.1 Manage VPN users using helper scripts

You may use helper scripts to add, delete or update VPN users for both IPsec/L2TP and IPsec/XAuth ("Cisco IPsec") modes. For IKEv2, see section 3.3 Manage IKEv2 clients.

Note: Replace command arguments below with your own values. VPN users are stored in `/etc/ppp/chap-secrets` and `/etc/ipsec.d/passwd`. The scripts will backup these files before making changes, with `.old-date-time` suffix.

9.1.1 Add or edit a VPN user

Add a new VPN user, or update an existing VPN user with a new password.

Run the helper script and follow the prompts:

```
sudo addvpnuser.sh
```

Alternatively, you can run the script with arguments:

```
# All values MUST be placed inside 'single quotes'
# DO NOT use these special characters within values: \ " '
sudo addvpnuser.sh 'username_to_add' 'password'
# OR
sudo addvpnuser.sh 'username_to_update' 'new_password'
```

9.1.2 Delete a VPN user

Delete the specified VPN user.

Run the helper script and follow the prompts:

```
sudo delvpnuser.sh
```

Alternatively, you can run the script with arguments:

```
# All values MUST be placed inside 'single quotes'
# DO NOT use these special characters within values: \ " '
sudo delvpnuser.sh 'username_to_delete'
```

9.1.3 Update all VPN users

Remove **all existing VPN users** and replace with the list of users you specify.

First, download the helper script:

```
wget https://get.vpnsetup.net/updateusers -O updateusers.sh
```

Important: This script will remove **all existing VPN users** and replace with the list of users you specify. Therefore, you must include any existing user(s) you want to keep in the variables below.

To use this script, choose one of the following options:

Option 1: Edit the script and enter VPN user details:

```
nano -w updateusers.sh
[Replace with your own values: YOUR_USERNAMES and YOUR_PASSWORDS]
sudo bash updateusers.sh
```

Option 2: Define VPN user details as environment variables:

```
# List of VPN usernames and passwords, separated by spaces
# All values MUST be placed inside 'single quotes'
# DO NOT use these special characters within values: \ " '
sudo \
```

```
VPN_USERS='username1 username2 ...' \
VPN_PASSWORDS='password1 password2 ...' \
bash updateusers.sh
```

9.2 View VPN users

By default, the VPN setup scripts will create the same VPN user for both IPsec/L2TP and IPsec/XAuth ("Cisco IPsec") modes.

For IPsec/L2TP, VPN users are specified in /etc/ppp/chap-secrets. The format of this file is:

```
"username1"  l2tpd  "password1"  *
"username2"  l2tpd  "password2"  *
... ...
```

For IPsec/XAuth ("Cisco IPsec"), VPN users are specified in /etc/ipsec.d/passwd. Passwords in this file are salted and hashed. See section 9.4 Manually manage VPN users for more details.

9.3 View or update the IPsec PSK

The IPsec PSK (pre-shared key) is stored in /etc/ipsec.secrets. All VPN users will share the same IPsec PSK. The format of this file is:

```
%any  %any  : PSK "your_ipsec_pre_shared_key"
```

To change to a new PSK, just edit this file. DO NOT use these special characters within values: \ " '

You must restart services when finished:

```
service ipsec restart
service xl2tpd restart
```

9.4 Manually manage VPN users

For IPsec/L2TP, VPN users are specified in `/etc/ppp/chap-secrets`. The format of this file is:

```
"username1"  l2tpd  "password1"  *
"username2"  l2tpd  "password2"  *
... ...
```

You can add more users, use one line for each user. DO NOT use these special characters within values: \ " '

For IPsec/XAuth ("Cisco IPsec"), VPN users are specified in `/etc/ipsec.d/passwd`. The format of this file is:

```
username1:password1hashed:xauth-psk
username2:password2hashed:xauth-psk
... ...
```

Passwords in this file are salted and hashed. This step can be done using e.g. the `openssl` utility:

```
# The output will be password1hashed
# Put your password inside 'single quotes'
openssl passwd -1 'password1'
```

10 IPsec VPN: Uninstall the VPN

- Uninstall using helper script
- Manually uninstall the VPN

10.1 Uninstall using helper script

To uninstall IPsec VPN, run the helper script:

Warning: This helper script will remove IPsec VPN from your server. All VPN configuration will be **permanently deleted**, and Libreswan and xl2tpd will be removed. This **cannot be undone**!

```
wget https://get.vpnsetup.net/unst -O unst.sh && sudo bash unst.sh
```

▼ If you are unable to download, follow the steps below.

You may also use `curl` to download:

```
curl -fsSL https://get.vpnsetup.net/unst -o unst.sh
sudo bash unst.sh
```

Alternative script URLs:

```
https://github.com/hwdsl2/setup-ipsec-
vpn/raw/master/extras/vpnuninstall.sh
https://gitlab.com/hwdsl2/setup-ipsec-
vpn/-/raw/master/extras/vpnuninstall.sh
```

10.2 Manually uninstall the VPN

Alternatively, you may manually uninstall IPsec VPN by following these steps. Commands must be run as `root`, or with `sudo`.

Warning: These steps will remove IPsec VPN from your server. All VPN configuration will be **permanently deleted**, and Libreswan and xl2tpd will be removed. This **cannot be undone**!

- First step
- Second step
- Third step
- Fourth step
- Optional
- When finished

10.2.0.1 First step

```
service ipsec stop
service xl2tpd stop
rm -rf /usr/local/sbin/ipsec /usr/local/libexec/ipsec \
       /usr/local/share/doc/libreswan
rm -f /etc/init/ipsec.conf /lib/systemd/system/ipsec.service \
      /etc/init.d/ipsec /usr/lib/systemd/system/ipsec.service \
      /etc/logrotate.d/libreswan \
      /usr/lib/tmpfiles.d/libreswan.conf
```

10.2.0.2 Second step

Ubuntu & Debian

```
apt-get purge xl2tpd
```

CentOS/RHEL, Rocky Linux, AlmaLinux, Oracle Linux & Amazon Linux 2

```
yum remove xl2tpd
```

Alpine Linux

```
apk del xl2tpd
```

10.2.0.3 Third step

Ubuntu, Debian & Alpine Linux

Edit `/etc/iptables.rules` and remove unneeded rules. Your original rules (if any) are backed up as `/etc/iptables.rules.old-date-time`. In addition, edit `/etc/iptables/rules.v4` if the file exists.

CentOS/RHEL, Rocky Linux, AlmaLinux, Oracle Linux & Amazon Linux 2

Edit `/etc/sysconfig/iptables` and remove unneeded rules. Your original rules (if any) are backed up as `/etc/sysconfig/iptables.old-date-time`.

Note: If using Rocky Linux, AlmaLinux, Oracle Linux 8 or CentOS/RHEL 8 and firewalld was active during VPN setup, nftables may be configured. Edit `/etc/sysconfig/nftables.conf` and remove unneeded rules. Your original rules are backed up as `/etc/sysconfig/nftables.conf.old-date-time`.

10.2.0.4 Fourth step

Edit `/etc/sysctl.conf` and remove the lines after `# Added by hwdsl2 VPN script`.
Edit `/etc/rc.local` and remove the lines after `# Added by hwdsl2 VPN script`. DO NOT remove `exit 0` (if any).

10.2.0.5 Optional

Note: This step is optional.

Remove these config files:

- /etc/ipsec.conf*
- /etc/ipsec.secrets*
- /etc/ppp/chap-secrets*
- /etc/ppp/options.xl2tpd*
- /etc/pam.d/pluto
- /etc/sysconfig/pluto
- /etc/default/pluto
- /etc/ipsec.d (directory)
- /etc/xl2tpd (directory)

```
rm -f /etc/ipsec.conf* /etc/ipsec.secrets* \
    /etc/ppp/chap-secrets* \
```

```
    /etc/ppp/options.xl2tpd* \
    /etc/pam.d/pluto /etc/sysconfig/pluto \
    /etc/default/pluto
rm -rf /etc/ipsec.d /etc/xl2tpd
```

Remove helper scripts:

```
rm -f /usr/bin/ikev2.sh /opt/src/ikev2.sh \
    /usr/bin/addvpnuser.sh /opt/src/addvpnuser.sh \
    /usr/bin/delvpnuser.sh /opt/src/delvpnuser.sh
```

Remove fail2ban:

Note: This is optional. Fail2ban can help protect SSH on your server. Removing it is NOT recommended.

```
service fail2ban stop
# Ubuntu & Debian
apt-get purge fail2ban
# CentOS/RHEL, Rocky Linux, AlmaLinux,
# Oracle Linux & Amazon Linux 2
yum remove fail2ban
# Alpine Linux
apk del fail2ban
```

10.2.0.6 When finished

Reboot your server.

11 Set Up Your Own IPsec VPN Server on Docker

View this project on the web: https://github.com/hwdsl2/docker-ipsec-vpn-server

Use this Docker image to run an IPsec VPN server, with IPsec/L2TP, Cisco IPsec and IKEv2.

This image is based on Alpine or Debian Linux with Libreswan (IPsec VPN software) and xl2tpd (L2TP daemon).

11.1 Features

- Supports IKEv2 with strong and fast ciphers (e.g. AES-GCM)
- Generates VPN profiles to auto-configure iOS, macOS and Android devices
- Supports Windows, macOS, iOS, Android, Chrome OS and Linux as VPN clients
- Includes a helper script to manage IKEv2 users and certificates

11.2 Quick start

Use this command to set up an IPsec VPN server on Docker:

```
docker run \
    --name ipsec-vpn-server \
    --restart=always \
    -v ikev2-vpn-data:/etc/ipsec.d \
    -v /lib/modules:/lib/modules:ro \
    -p 500:500/udp \
    -p 4500:4500/udp \
    -d --privileged \
    hwdsl2/ipsec-vpn-server
```

Your VPN login details will be randomly generated. See section 11.5.3 Retrieve VPN login details.

To learn more about how to use this image, read the sections below.

11.3 Install Docker

First, install Docker (https://docs.docker.com/engine/install/) on your Linux server. You may also use Podman to run this image, after creating an alias (https://podman.io/whatis.html) for `docker`.

Advanced users can use this image on macOS with Docker for Mac. Before using IPsec/L2TP mode, you may need to restart the Docker container once with `docker restart ipsec-vpn-server`. This image does not support Docker for Windows.

11.4 Download

Get the trusted build from the Docker Hub registry (https://hub.docker.com/r/hwdsl2/ipsec-vpn-server/):

```
docker pull hwdsl2/ipsec-vpn-server
```

Alternatively, you may download from Quay.io (https://quay.io/repository/hwdsl2/ipsec-vpn-server):

```
docker pull quay.io/hwdsl2/ipsec-vpn-server
docker image tag quay.io/hwdsl2/ipsec-vpn-server \
  hwdsl2/ipsec-vpn-server
```

Supported platforms: `linux/amd64`, `linux/arm64` and `linux/arm/v7`.

Advanced users can build from source code on GitHub. See section 12.11 for more details.

11.4.1 Image comparison

Two pre-built images are available. At the time of writing, the default Alpine-based image is only ~17MB.

	Alpine-based	**Debian-based**
Image name	hwdsl2/ipsec-vpn-server	hwdsl2/ipsec-vpn-server:debian
Compressed size	~ 17 MB	~ 63 MB
Base image	Alpine Linux	Debian Linux
Platforms	amd64, arm64, arm/v7	amd64, arm64, arm/v7
IPsec/L2TP	✔	✔
Cisco IPsec	✔	✔
IKEv2	✔	✔

Note: To use the Debian-based image, replace every `hwdsl2/ipsec-vpn-server` with `hwdsl2/ipsec-vpn-server:debian` in this chapter.

11.5 How to use this image

11.5.1 Environment variables

Note: All the variables to this image are optional, which means you don't have to type in any variable, and you can have an IPsec VPN server out of the box! To do that, create an empty env file using `touch vpn.env`, and skip to the next section.

This Docker image uses the following variables, that can be declared in an env file. See section 11.11 for an example env file.

```
VPN_IPSEC_PSK=your_ipsec_pre_shared_key
VPN_USER=your_vpn_username
VPN_PASSWORD=your_vpn_password
```

This will create a user account for VPN login, which can be used by your multiple devices. The IPsec PSK (pre-shared key) is specified by the `VPN_IPSEC_PSK` environment variable. The VPN username is defined in `VPN_USER`, and VPN password is specified by `VPN_PASSWORD`.

Additional VPN users are supported, and can be optionally declared in your env file like this. Usernames and passwords must be separated by spaces, and usernames cannot contain duplicates. All VPN users will share the same IPsec PSK.

```
VPN_ADDL_USERS=additional_username_1 additional_username_2
VPN_ADDL_PASSWORDS=additional_password_1 additional_password_2
```

Note: In your env file, DO NOT put "" or ' ' around values, or add space around =. DO NOT use these special characters within values: \ " '. A secure IPsec PSK should consist of at least 20 random characters.

Note: If you modify the env file after the Docker container is already created, you must remove and re-create the container for the changes to take effect. Refer to section 11.8 Update Docker image.

▼ You may optionally specify a DNS name, client name and/or custom DNS servers.

Advanced users can optionally specify a DNS name for the IKEv2 server address. The DNS name must be a fully qualified domain name (FQDN). Example:

```
VPN_DNS_NAME=vpn.example.com
```

You may specify a name for the first IKEv2 client. Use one word only, no special characters except – and _. The default is `vpnclient` if not specified.

```
VPN_CLIENT_NAME=your_client_name
```

By default, clients are set to use Google Public DNS when the VPN is active. You may specify custom DNS server(s) for all VPN modes. Example:

```
VPN_DNS_SRV1=1.1.1.1
VPN_DNS_SRV2=1.0.0.1
```

By default, no password is required when importing IKEv2 client configuration. You can choose to protect client config files using a random password.

```
VPN_PROTECT_CONFIG=yes
```

Note: The variables above have no effect for IKEv2 mode, if IKEv2 is already set up in the Docker container. In this case, you may remove IKEv2 and set it up again using custom options. Refer to section 11.9 Configure and use IKEv2 VPN.

11.5.2 Start the IPsec VPN server

Create a new Docker container from this image (replace `./vpn.env` with your own env file):

```
docker run \
    --name ipsec-vpn-server \
    --env-file ./vpn.env \
    --restart=always \
    -v ikev2-vpn-data:/etc/ipsec.d \
    -v /lib/modules:/lib/modules:ro \
    -p 500:500/udp \
    -p 4500:4500/udp \
    -d --privileged \
    hwdsl2/ipsec-vpn-server
```

In this command, we use the -v option of `docker run` to create a new Docker volume named `ikev2-vpn-data`, and mount it into `/etc/ipsec.d` in the container. IKEv2 related data such as certificates and keys will persist in the volume, and later when you need to re-create the Docker container, just specify the same volume again.

It is recommended to enable IKEv2 when using this image. However, if you prefer not to enable IKEv2 and use only the IPsec/L2TP and IPsec/XAuth ("Cisco IPsec") modes to connect to the VPN, remove the first -v option from the `docker run` command above.

Note: Advanced users can also run without privileged mode. See section 12.2 for more details.

11.5.3 Retrieve VPN login details

If you did not specify an `env` file in the `docker run` command above, `VPN_USER` will default to `vpnuser` and both `VPN_IPSEC_PSK` and `VPN_PASSWORD` will be randomly generated. To retrieve them, view the container logs:

```
docker logs ipsec-vpn-server
```

Search for these lines in the output:

```
Connect to your new VPN with these details:

Server IP: your_vpn_server_ip
IPsec PSK: your_ipsec_pre_shared_key
Username: your_vpn_username
Password: your_vpn_password
```

The output will also include details for IKEv2 mode, if enabled.

(Optional) Backup the generated VPN login details (if any) to the current directory:

```
docker cp ipsec-vpn-server:/etc/ipsec.d/vpn-gen.env ./
```

11.6 Next steps

Get your computer or device to use the VPN. Please refer to:

11.9 Configure and use IKEv2 VPN (recommended)
5 Configure IPsec/L2TP VPN Clients
6 Configure IPsec/XAuth ("Cisco IPsec") VPN Clients

Enjoy your very own VPN!

11.7 Important notes

Windows users: For IPsec/L2TP mode, a one-time registry change (see section 7.3.1) is required if the VPN server or client is behind NAT (e.g. home router).

The same VPN account can be used by your multiple devices. However, due to an IPsec/L2TP limitation, if you wish to connect multiple devices from behind the same NAT (e.g. home router), you must use IKEv2 or IPsec/XAuth mode.

If you wish to add, edit or remove VPN user accounts, first update your env file, then you must remove and re-create the Docker container using instructions from the next section. Advanced users can bind mount the env file. See section 12.13 for more details.

For servers with an external firewall (e.g. EC2/GCE), open UDP ports 500 and 4500 for the VPN.

Clients are set to use Google Public DNS when the VPN is active. If another DNS provider is preferred, read section 12.1 Use alternative DNS servers.

11.8 Update Docker image

To update the Docker image and container, first download the latest version:

```
docker pull hwdsl2/ipsec-vpn-server
```

If the Docker image is already up to date, you should see:

```
Status: Image is up to date for hwdsl2/ipsec-vpn-server:latest
```

Otherwise, it will download the latest version. To update your Docker container, first write down all your VPN login details (see section 11.5.3). Then remove the Docker container with `docker rm -f ipsec-vpn-server`. Finally, re-create it using instructions from section 11.5 How to use this image.

11.9 Configure and use IKEv2 VPN

IKEv2 mode has improvements over IPsec/L2TP and IPsec/XAuth ("Cisco IPsec"), and does not require an IPsec PSK, username or password. Read more in chapter 3, Guide: How to Set Up and Use IKEv2 VPN.

First, check container logs to view details for IKEv2:

```
docker logs ipsec-vpn-server
```

Note: If you cannot find IKEv2 details, IKEv2 may not be enabled in the container. Try updating the Docker image and container using instructions from section 11.8 Update Docker image.

During IKEv2 setup, an IKEv2 client (with default name vpnclient) is created, with its configuration exported to /etc/ipsec.d **inside the container**. To copy config file(s) to the Docker host:

```
# Check contents of /etc/ipsec.d in the container
docker exec -it ipsec-vpn-server ls -l /etc/ipsec.d
# Example: Copy a client config file from the container
# to the current directory on the Docker host
docker cp ipsec-vpn-server:/etc/ipsec.d/vpnclient.p12 ./
```

Next steps: Configure your devices to use the IKEv2 VPN. See section 3.2 for more details.

▼ Learn how to manage IKEv2 clients.

You can manage IKEv2 clients using the helper script. See examples below. To customize client options, run the script without arguments.

```
# Add a new client (using default options)
docker exec -it ipsec-vpn-server ikev2.sh \
  --addclient [client name]
# Export configuration for an existing client
docker exec -it ipsec-vpn-server ikev2.sh \
  --exportclient [client name]
# List existing clients
docker exec -it ipsec-vpn-server ikev2.sh --listclients
```

```
# Show usage
docker exec -it ipsec-vpn-server ikev2.sh -h
```

Note: If you encounter error "executable file not found", replace `ikev2.sh` above with `/opt/src/ikev2.sh`.

▼ Learn how to change the IKEv2 server address.

In certain circumstances, you may need to change the IKEv2 server address. For example, to switch to use a DNS name, or after server IP changes. To change the IKEv2 server address, first open a bash shell inside the container (see section 12.12), then follow instructions in section 3.4. Note that the container logs will not show the new IKEv2 server address until you restart the Docker container.

▼ Remove IKEv2 and set it up again using custom options.

In certain circumstances, you may need to remove IKEv2 and set it up again using custom options.

Warning: All IKEv2 configuration including certificates and keys will be **permanently deleted**. This **cannot be undone**!

Option 1: Remove IKEv2 and set it up again using the helper script.

Note that this will override variables you specified in the env file, such as `VPN_DNS_NAME` and `VPN_CLIENT_NAME`, and the container logs will no longer show up-to-date information for IKEv2.

```
# Remove IKEv2 and delete all IKEv2 configuration
docker exec -it ipsec-vpn-server ikev2.sh --removeikev2
# Set up IKEv2 again using custom options
docker exec -it ipsec-vpn-server ikev2.sh
```

Option 2: Remove `ikev2-vpn-data` and re-create the container.

1. Write down all your VPN login details (see section 11.5.3).
2. Remove the Docker container: `docker rm -f ipsec-vpn-server`.
3. Remove the `ikev2-vpn-data` volume: `docker volume rm ikev2-vpn-data`.
4. Update your env file and add custom IKEv2 options such as `VPN_DNS_NAME` and `VPN_CLIENT_NAME`, then re-create the container. Refer

to section 11.5 How to use this image.

11.10 Technical details

There are two services running: Libreswan (pluto) for the IPsec VPN, and xl2tpd for L2TP support.

The default IPsec configuration supports:

- IPsec/L2TP with PSK
- IKEv1 with PSK and XAuth ("Cisco IPsec")
- IKEv2

The ports that are exposed for this container to work are:

- 4500/udp and 500/udp for IPsec

11.11 Example VPN env file

```
# Note: All the variables to this image are optional.
#        See section 11.5 for more details.


# Define IPsec PSK, VPN username and password
# - DO NOT put "" or '' around values, or add space around =
# - DO NOT use these special characters within values: \ " '
VPN_IPSEC_PSK=your_ipsec_pre_shared_key
VPN_USER=your_vpn_username
VPN_PASSWORD=your_vpn_password


# Define additional VPN users
# - DO NOT put "" or '' around values, or add space around =
# - DO NOT use these special characters within values: \ " '
# - Usernames and passwords must be separated by spaces
VPN_ADDL_USERS=additional_username_1 additional_username_2
VPN_ADDL_PASSWORDS=additional_password_1 additional_password_2


# Use a DNS name for the VPN server
```

```
# - The DNS name must be a fully qualified domain name (FQDN)
VPN_DNS_NAME=vpn.example.com

# Specify a name for the first IKEv2 client
# - Use one word only, no special characters except '-' and '_'
# - The default is 'vpnclient' if not specified
VPN_CLIENT_NAME=your_client_name

# Use alternative DNS servers
# - By default, clients are set to use Google Public DNS
# - Example below shows Cloudflare's DNS service
VPN_DNS_SRV1=1.1.1.1
VPN_DNS_SRV2=1.0.0.1

# Protect IKEv2 client config files using a password
# - By default, no password is required when importing IKEv2
#   client configuration
# - Set this variable if you want to protect these files
#   using a random password
VPN_PROTECT_CONFIG=yes
```

12 Docker VPN: Advanced Usage

- Use alternative DNS servers
- Run without privileged mode
- Select VPN modes
- Access other containers on the Docker host
- Specify VPN server's public IP
- Assign static IPs to VPN clients
- Customize VPN subnets
- About host network mode
- Enable Libreswan logs
- Check server status
- Build from source code
- Bash shell inside container
- Bind mount the env file
- Deploy Google BBR congestion control

12.1 Use alternative DNS servers

Clients are set to use Google Public DNS: https://developers.google.com/speed/public-dns/ when the VPN is active. If another DNS provider is preferred, define `VPN_DNS_SRV1` and optionally `VPN_DNS_SRV2` in your env file, then follow instructions in section 11.8 to recreate the Docker container. For example, if you want to use Cloudflare's DNS service (https://1.1.1.1/dns/):

```
VPN_DNS_SRV1=1.1.1.1
VPN_DNS_SRV2=1.0.0.1
```

Note that if IKEv2 is already set up in the Docker container, you will also need to edit `/etc/ipsec.d/ikev2.conf` inside the Docker container and replace `8.8.8.8` and `8.8.4.4` with your alternative DNS server(s), then restart the Docker container.

12.2 Run without privileged mode

Advanced users can create a Docker container from this image without using privileged mode (replace `./vpn.env` in the command below with your own env file).

Note: If your Docker host runs CentOS Stream, Oracle Linux 8+, Rocky Linux or AlmaLinux, it is recommended to use privileged mode (see section 11.5.2). If you want to run without privileged mode, you **must** run `modprobe ip_tables` before creating the Docker container and also on boot.

```
docker run \
    --name ipsec-vpn-server \
    --env-file ./vpn.env \
    --restart=always \
    -v ikev2-vpn-data:/etc/ipsec.d \
    -p 500:500/udp \
    -p 4500:4500/udp \
    -d --cap-add=NET_ADMIN \
    --device=/dev/ppp \
    --sysctl net.ipv4.ip_forward=1 \
    --sysctl net.ipv4.conf.all.accept_redirects=0 \
    --sysctl net.ipv4.conf.all.send_redirects=0 \
    --sysctl net.ipv4.conf.all.rp_filter=0 \
    --sysctl net.ipv4.conf.default.accept_redirects=0 \
    --sysctl net.ipv4.conf.default.send_redirects=0 \
    --sysctl net.ipv4.conf.default.rp_filter=0 \
    --sysctl net.ipv4.conf.eth0.send_redirects=0 \
    --sysctl net.ipv4.conf.eth0.rp_filter=0 \
    hwdsl2/ipsec-vpn-server
```

When running without privileged mode, the container is unable to change `sysctl` settings. This could affect certain features of this image. A known issue is that the Android/Linux MTU/MSS fix (section 7.3.6) also requires adding `--sysctl net.ipv4.ip_no_pmtu_disc=1` to the docker run command. If you encounter any issues, try re-creating the container using privileged mode (see section 11.5.2).

After creating the Docker container, see section 11.5.3 Retrieve VPN login details.

Similarly, if using Docker compose, you may replace `privileged: true` in https://github.com/hwdsl2/docker-ipsec-vpn-server/blob/master/docker-compose.yml with:

```
cap_add:
  - NET_ADMIN
devices:
  - "/dev/ppp:/dev/ppp"
sysctls:
  - net.ipv4.ip_forward=1
  - net.ipv4.conf.all.accept_redirects=0
  - net.ipv4.conf.all.send_redirects=0
  - net.ipv4.conf.all.rp_filter=0
  - net.ipv4.conf.default.accept_redirects=0
  - net.ipv4.conf.default.send_redirects=0
  - net.ipv4.conf.default.rp_filter=0
  - net.ipv4.conf.eth0.send_redirects=0
  - net.ipv4.conf.eth0.rp_filter=0
```

For more information, see compose file reference: https://docs.docker.com/compose/compose-file/

12.3 Select VPN modes

Using this Docker image, the IPsec/L2TP and IPsec/XAuth ("Cisco IPsec") modes are enabled by default. In addition, IKEv2 mode will be enabled if the `-v ikev2-vpn-data:/etc/ipsec.d` option is specified in the `docker run` command when creating the Docker container. Refer to section 11.5.2.

Advanced users can selectively disable VPN modes by setting the following variable(s) in the env file, then re-create the Docker container.

Disable IPsec/L2TP mode: `VPN_DISABLE_IPSEC_L2TP=yes`
Disable IPsec/XAuth ("Cisco IPsec") mode: `VPN_DISABLE_IPSEC_XAUTH=yes`
Disable both IPsec/L2TP and IPsec/XAuth modes: `VPN_IKEV2_ONLY=yes`

12.4 Access other containers on the Docker host

After connecting to the VPN, VPN clients can generally access services running in other containers on the same Docker host, without additional configuration.

For example, if the IPsec VPN server container has IP `172.17.0.2`, and an Nginx container with IP `172.17.0.3` is running on the same Docker host, VPN clients can use IP `172.17.0.3` to access services on the Nginx container. To find out which IP is assigned to a container, run `docker inspect <container name>`.

12.5 Specify VPN server's public IP

On Docker hosts with multiple public IP addresses, advanced users can specify a public IP for the VPN server using variable `VPN_PUBLIC_IP` in the env file, then re-create the Docker container. For example, if the Docker host has IPs `192.0.2.1` and `192.0.2.2`, and you want the VPN server to use `192.0.2.2`:

```
VPN_PUBLIC_IP=192.0.2.2
```

Note that this variable has no effect for IKEv2 mode, if IKEv2 is already set up in the Docker container. In this case, you may remove IKEv2 and set it up again using custom options. Refer to section 11.9 Configure and use IKEv2 VPN.

Additional configuration may be required if you want VPN clients to use the specified public IP as their "outgoing IP" when the VPN connection is active, and the specified IP is NOT the main IP (or default route) on the Docker host. In this case, you can try adding an IPTables `SNAT` rule on the Docker host. To persist after reboot, you may add the command to `/etc/rc.local`.

Continuing with the example above, if the Docker container has internal IP `172.17.0.2` (check using `docker inspect ipsec-vpn-server`), Docker's network interface name is `docker0` (check using `iptables -nvL -t nat`), and you want the "outgoing IP" to be `192.0.2.2`:

```
iptables -t nat -I POSTROUTING -s 172.17.0.2 ! -o docker0 \
  -j SNAT --to 192.0.2.2
```

To check the "outgoing IP" for a connected VPN client, you may open a browser on the client and look up the IP address on Google.

12.6 Assign static IPs to VPN clients

When connecting using IPsec/L2TP mode, the VPN server (Docker container) has internal IP 192.168.42.1 within the VPN subnet 192.168.42.0/24. Clients are assigned internal IPs from 192.168.42.10 to 192.168.42.250. To check which IP is assigned to a client, view the connection status on the VPN client.

When connecting using IPsec/XAuth ("Cisco IPsec") or IKEv2 mode, the VPN server (Docker container) does NOT have an internal IP within the VPN subnet 192.168.43.0/24. Clients are assigned internal IPs from 192.168.43.10 to 192.168.43.250.

Advanced users may optionally assign static IPs to VPN clients. IKEv2 mode does NOT support this feature. To assign static IPs, declare the VPN_ADDL_IP_ADDRS variable in your env file, then re-create the Docker container. Example:

```
VPN_ADDL_USERS=user1 user2 user3 user4 user5
VPN_ADDL_PASSWORDS=pass1 pass2 pass3 pass4 pass5
VPN_ADDL_IP_ADDRS=* * 192.168.42.2 192.168.43.2
```

In this example, we assign static IP 192.168.42.2 for user3 for IPsec/L2TP mode, and assign static IP 192.168.43.2 for user4 for IPsec/XAuth ("Cisco IPsec") mode. Internal IPs for user1, user2 and user5 will be auto-assigned. The internal IP for user3 for IPsec/XAuth mode and the internal IP for user4 for IPsec/L2TP mode will also be auto-assigned. You may use * to specify auto-assigned IPs, or put those user(s) at the end of the list.

Static IPs that you specify for IPsec/L2TP mode must be within the range from 192.168.42.2 to 192.168.42.9. Static IPs that you specify for IPsec/XAuth ("Cisco IPsec") mode must be within the range from 192.168.43.2 to 192.168.43.9.

If you need to assign more static IPs, you must shrink the pool of auto-assigned IP addresses. Example:

```
VPN_L2TP_POOL=192.168.42.100-192.168.42.250
VPN_XAUTH_POOL=192.168.43.100-192.168.43.250
```

This will allow you to assign static IPs within the range from `192.168.42.2` to `192.168.42.99` for IPsec/L2TP mode, and within the range from `192.168.43.2` to `192.168.43.99` for IPsec/XAuth ("Cisco IPsec") mode.

Note that if you specify `VPN_XAUTH_POOL` in the env file, and IKEv2 is already set up in the Docker container, you **must** manually edit `/etc/ipsec.d/ikev2.conf` inside the container and replace `rightaddresspool=192.168.43.10-192.168.43.250` with the **same value** as `VPN_XAUTH_POOL`, before re-creating the Docker container. Otherwise, IKEv2 may stop working.

Note: In your env file, DO NOT put "" or ' ' around values, or add space around =. DO NOT use these special characters within values: \ " '.

12.7 Customize VPN subnets

By default, IPsec/L2TP VPN clients will use internal VPN subnet `192.168.42.0/24`, while IPsec/XAuth ("Cisco IPsec") and IKEv2 VPN clients will use internal VPN subnet `192.168.43.0/24`. For more details, read the previous section.

For most use cases, it is NOT necessary and NOT recommended to customize these subnets. If your use case requires it, however, you may specify custom subnet(s) in your env file, then you must re-create the Docker container.

```
# Example: Specify custom VPN subnet for IPsec/L2TP mode
# Note: All three variables must be specified.
VPN_L2TP_NET=10.1.0.0/16
VPN_L2TP_LOCAL=10.1.0.1
VPN_L2TP_POOL=10.1.0.10-10.1.254.254

# Example: Specify custom VPN subnet for IPsec/XAuth
#          and IKEv2 modes
```

```
# Note: Both variables must be specified.
VPN_XAUTH_NET=10.2.0.0/16
VPN_XAUTH_POOL=10.2.0.10-10.2.254.254
```

Note: In your env file, DO NOT put "" or '' around values, or add space around =.

In the examples above, `VPN_L2TP_LOCAL` is the VPN server's internal IP for IPsec/L2TP mode. `VPN_L2TP_POOL` and `VPN_XAUTH_POOL` are the pools of auto-assigned IP addresses for VPN clients.

Note that if you specify `VPN_XAUTH_POOL` in the env file, and IKEv2 is already set up in the Docker container, you **must** manually edit `/etc/ipsec.d/ikev2.conf` inside the container and replace `rightaddresspool=192.168.43.10-192.168.43.250` with the **same value** as `VPN_XAUTH_POOL`, before re-creating the Docker container. Otherwise, IKEv2 may stop working.

12.8 About host network mode

Advanced users can run this image in host network mode (https://docs.docker.com/network/host/), by adding `--network=host` to the `docker run` command. In addition, if running without privileged mode (see section 12.2), you may also need to replace `eth0` with the network interface name of your Docker host.

Host network mode is NOT recommended for this image, unless your use case requires it. In this mode, the container's network stack is not isolated from the Docker host, and VPN clients may be able to access ports or services on the Docker host using its internal VPN IP `192.168.42.1` after connecting using IPsec/L2TP mode. Note that you will need to manually clean up the changes to IPTables rules and sysctl settings by run.sh (https://github.com/hwdsl2/docker-ipsec-vpn-server/blob/master/run.sh) or reboot the server when you no longer use this image.

Some Docker host OS, such as Debian 10, cannot run this image in host network mode due to the use of nftables.

12.9 Enable Libreswan logs

To keep the Docker image small, Libreswan (IPsec) logs are not enabled by default. If you need to enable it for troubleshooting purposes, first start a Bash session in the running container:

```
docker exec -it ipsec-vpn-server env TERM=xterm bash -l
```

Then run the following commands:

```
# For Alpine-based image
apk add --no-cache rsyslog
rsyslogd
rc-service ipsec stop; rc-service -D ipsec start >/dev/null 2>&1
sed -i '/pluto\.pid/a rsyslogd' /opt/src/run.sh
exit
# For Debian-based image
apt-get update && apt-get -y install rsyslog
rsyslogd
service ipsec restart
sed -i '/pluto\.pid/a rsyslogd' /opt/src/run.sh
exit
```

Note: The error `rsyslogd: imklog: cannot open kernel log` is normal if you use this Docker image without privileged mode.

When finished, you may check Libreswan logs with:

```
docker exec -it ipsec-vpn-server grep pluto /var/log/auth.log
```

To check xl2tpd logs, run `docker logs ipsec-vpn-server`.

12.10 Check server status

Check the status of the IPsec VPN server:

```
docker exec -it ipsec-vpn-server ipsec status
```

Show currently established VPN connections:

```
docker exec -it ipsec-vpn-server ipsec trafficstatus
```

12.11 Build from source code

Advanced users can download and compile the source code from GitHub:

```
git clone https://github.com/hwdsl2/docker-ipsec-vpn-server
cd docker-ipsec-vpn-server
# To build Alpine-based image
docker build -t hwdsl2/ipsec-vpn-server .
# To build Debian-based image
docker build -f Dockerfile.debian \
  -t hwdsl2/ipsec-vpn-server:debian .
```

Or use this if not modifying the source code:

```
# To build Alpine-based image
docker build -t hwdsl2/ipsec-vpn-server \
  github.com/hwdsl2/docker-ipsec-vpn-server
# To build Debian-based image
docker build -f Dockerfile.debian \
  -t hwdsl2/ipsec-vpn-server:debian \
  github.com/hwdsl2/docker-ipsec-vpn-server
```

12.12 Bash shell inside container

To start a Bash session in the running container:

```
docker exec -it ipsec-vpn-server env TERM=xterm bash -l
```

(Optional) Install the nano editor:

```
# For Alpine-based image
apk add --no-cache nano
# For Debian-based image
apt-get update && apt-get -y install nano
```

Then run your commands inside the container. When finished, exit the container and restart if needed:

```
exit
docker restart ipsec-vpn-server
```

12.13 Bind mount the env file

As an alternative to the `--env-file` option, advanced users can bind mount the env file. The advantage of this method is that after updating the env file, you can restart the Docker container to take effect instead of re-creating it. To use this method, you must first edit your env file and use single quotes `' '` to enclose the values of all variables. Then (re-)create the Docker container (replace the first `vpn.env` with your own env file):

```
docker run \
    --name ipsec-vpn-server \
    --restart=always \
    -v "$(pwd)/vpn.env:/opt/src/env/vpn.env:ro" \
    -v ikev2-vpn-data:/etc/ipsec.d \
    -v /lib/modules:/lib/modules:ro \
    -p 500:500/udp \
    -p 4500:4500/udp \
    -d --privileged \
    hwdsl2/ipsec-vpn-server
```

12.14 Deploy Google BBR congestion control

After the VPN server is set up, the performance can be improved by deploying the Google BBR congestion control algorithm on your Docker host.

This is usually done by modifying the configuration file `/etc/sysctl.conf`. However, some Linux distributions may additionally require updates to the Linux kernel.

115

For detailed deployment methods, please refer to:
https://github.com/hwdsl2/setup-ipsec-vpn/blob/master/docs/bbr.md

When finished, restart the Docker container:

```
docker restart ipsec-vpn-server
```

13 Set Up Your Own OpenVPN Server Using Auto Setup Script

View this project on the web: https://github.com/hwdsl2/openvpn-install

Use this OpenVPN server install script to set up your own VPN server in just a few minutes, even if you haven't used OpenVPN before. OpenVPN is an open-source, robust and highly flexible VPN protocol.

This script supports Ubuntu, Debian, AlmaLinux, Rocky Linux, CentOS, Fedora, openSUSE, Amazon Linux 2 and Raspberry Pi OS.

13.1 Features

- Fully automated OpenVPN server setup, no user input needed
- Supports interactive install using custom options
- Generates VPN profiles to auto-configure Windows, macOS, iOS and Android devices
- Supports managing OpenVPN users and certificates
- Optimizes `sysctl` settings for improved VPN performance

13.2 Installation

First, download the script on your Linux server*:

```
wget -O openvpn.sh https://get.vpnsetup.net/ovpn
```

* A cloud server, virtual private server (VPS) or dedicated server.

Option 1: Auto install OpenVPN using default options.

```
sudo bash openvpn.sh --auto
```

For servers with an external firewall (e.g. EC2/GCE), open UDP port 1194 for the VPN.

117

Option 2: Interactive install using custom options.

```
sudo bash openvpn.sh
```

You can customize the following options: VPN server's DNS name, protocol (TCP/UDP) and port, DNS server for VPN clients and name of the first client.

For servers with an external firewall, open your selected TCP or UDP port for the VPN.

▼ If you are unable to download, follow the steps below.

You may also use `curl` to download:

```
curl -fL -o openvpn.sh https://get.vpnsetup.net/ovpn
```

Then follow the instructions above to install.

Alternative setup URLs:

```
https://github.com/hwdsl2/openvpn-install/raw/master/openvpn-install.sh
https://gitlab.com/hwdsl2/openvpn-install/-/raw/master/openvpn-install.sh
```

▼ Advanced: Auto install using custom options.

Advanced users can auto install OpenVPN using custom options, by providing a Bash "here document" as input to the setup script. This method can also be used to provide input to manage users after install.

First, install OpenVPN interactively using custom options, and write down all your inputs to the script.

```
sudo bash openvpn.sh
```

If you need to remove OpenVPN, run the script again and select the appropriate option.

Next, create the custom install command using your inputs. Example:

```
sudo bash openvpn.sh <<ANSWERS
n
1
1194
2
client
y
ANSWERS
```

Note: The install options may change in future versions of the script.

13.3 Next steps

After setup, you can run the script again to manage users or uninstall OpenVPN.

Get your computer or device to use the VPN. Please refer to:

14 Configure OpenVPN Clients

Enjoy your very own VPN!

14 Configure OpenVPN Clients

OpenVPN clients (https://openvpn.net/vpn-client/) are available for Windows, macOS, iOS, Android and Linux. macOS users can also use Tunnelblick (https://tunnelblick.net).

To add a VPN connection, first securely transfer the generated `.ovpn` file to your device, then open the OpenVPN App and import the VPN profile.

To manage OpenVPN clients, run the install script again: `sudo bash openvpn.sh`. See Chapter 15 for more details.

- Platforms
  - Windows
  - OS X (macOS)
  - Android
  - iOS (iPhone/iPad)

OpenVPN clients: https://openvpn.net/vpn-client/

14.1 Windows

1. Securely transfer the generated `.ovpn` file to your computer.
2. Install and launch the **OpenVPN Connect** VPN client.
3. On the **Import Profile** screen, click the **File** tab.
4. Drag and drop the `.ovpn` file into the window, or browse to and select the `.ovpn` file, then click **Open**.
5. Click **Connect**.

14.2 OS X (macOS)

1. Securely transfer the generated `.ovpn` file to your computer.
2. Install and launch Tunnelblick (https://tunnelblick.net).
3. On the welcome screen, click **I have configuration files**.

4. On the **Add a Configuration** screen, click **OK**.

5. Click the Tunnelblick icon in the menu bar, then select **VPN Details**.

6. Drag and drop the `.ovpn` file into the **Configurations** window (left pane).

7. Follow on-screen instructions to install the OpenVPN profile.

8. Click **Connect**.

14.3 Android

1. Securely transfer the generated `.ovpn` file to your Android device.

2. Install and launch **OpenVPN Connect** from **Google Play**.

3. On the **Import Profile** screen, tap the **File** tab.

4. Tap **Browse**, then browse to and select the `.ovpn` file.
   Note: To find the `.ovpn` file, tap the three-line menu button, then browse to the location you saved the file.

5. On the **Imported Profile** screen, tap **Add**.

6. Tap the new OpenVPN profile to connect.

14.4 iOS (iPhone/iPad)

First, install and launch **OpenVPN Connect** from **App Store**. Then securely transfer the generated `.ovpn` file to your iOS device. To transfer the file, you may use:

1. AirDrop the file and open with OpenVPN, or

2. Upload to your device (OpenVPN App folder) using File Sharing (https://support.apple.com/en-us/HT210598), then launch the OpenVPN Connect App and tap the **File** tab.

When finished, tap **Add** to import the VPN profile, then tap **Connect**.

To customize settings for the OpenVPN Connect App, tap the three-line menu button, then tap **Settings**.

15 OpenVPN: Manage VPN Clients

After setting up OpenVPN on your server, you can manage OpenVPN clients by following the instructions in this chapter. For example, you can add new VPN client(s) on the server for your additional computers and mobile devices, list existing clients, or export configuration for an existing client.

To manage OpenVPN clients, first connect to your server using SSH, then run:

```
sudo bash openvpn.sh
```

You will see the following options:

```
OpenVPN is already installed.

Select an option:
 1) Add a new client
 2) Export config for an existing client
 3) List existing clients
 4) Revoke an existing client
 5) Remove OpenVPN
 6) Exit
Option:
```

You can then enter your desired option to add, export, list or revoke OpenVPN client(s).

Note: These options may change in newer versions of the script. Read carefully before selecting your desired option.

15.1 Add a new client

To add a new OpenVPN client:

1. Select option 1 from the menu, by typing 1 and pressing enter.
2. Provide a name for the new client.

Next steps: Configure OpenVPN clients. See Chapter 14 for more details.

15.2 Export an existing client

To export OpenVPN configuration for an existing client:

1. Select option 2 from the menu, by typing 2 and pressing enter.
2. From the list of existing clients, select the client you want to export.

15.3 List existing clients

Select option 3 from the menu, by typing 3 and pressing enter. The script will then display a list of existing OpenVPN clients.

15.4 Revoke a client

In certain circumstances, you may need to revoke a previously generated OpenVPN client certificate.

1. Select option 4 from the menu, by typing 4 and pressing enter.
2. From the list of existing clients, select the client you want to revoke.
3. Confirm the client revocation.

16 Set Up Your Own WireGuard VPN Server Using Auto Setup Script

View this project on the web: https://github.com/hwdsl2/wireguard-install

Use this WireGuard VPN server install script to set up your own VPN server in just a few minutes, even if you haven't used WireGuard before. WireGuard is a fast and modern VPN designed with the goals of ease of use and high performance.

This script supports Ubuntu, Debian, AlmaLinux, Rocky Linux, CentOS, Fedora, openSUSE and Raspberry Pi OS.

16.1 Features

- Fully automated WireGuard VPN server setup, no user input needed
- Supports interactive install using custom options
- Generates VPN profiles to auto-configure Windows, macOS, iOS and Android devices
- Supports managing WireGuard VPN users
- Optimizes `sysctl` settings for improved VPN performance

16.2 Installation

First, download the script on your Linux server*:

```
wget -O wireguard.sh https://get.vpnsetup.net/wg
```

* A cloud server, virtual private server (VPS) or dedicated server.

Option 1: Auto install WireGuard using default options.

```
sudo bash wireguard.sh --auto
```

For servers with an external firewall (e.g. EC2/GCE), open UDP port 51820 for the VPN.

Option 2: Interactive install using custom options.

```
sudo bash wireguard.sh
```

You can customize the following options: VPN server's DNS name, UDP port, DNS server for VPN clients and name of the first client.

For servers with an external firewall, open your selected UDP port for the VPN.

▼ If you are unable to download, follow the steps below.

You may also use `curl` to download:

```
curl -fL -o wireguard.sh https://get.vpnsetup.net/wg
```

Then follow the instructions above to install.

Alternative setup URLs:

```
https://github.com/hwdsl2/wireguard-install/raw/master/wireguard-
install.sh
https://gitlab.com/hwdsl2/wireguard-
install/-/raw/master/wireguard-install.sh
```

▼ Advanced: Auto install using custom options.

Advanced users can auto install WireGuard using custom options, by providing a Bash "here document" as input to the setup script. This method can also be used to provide input to manage users after install.

First, install WireGuard interactively using custom options, and write down all your inputs to the script.

```
sudo bash wireguard.sh
```

If you need to remove WireGuard, run the script again and select the appropriate option.

Next, create the custom install command using your inputs. Example:

```
sudo bash wireguard.sh <<ANSWERS
n
51820
client
2
y
ANSWERS
```

Note: The install options may change in future versions of the script.

16.3 Next steps

After setup, you can run the script again to manage users or uninstall WireGuard.

Get your computer or device to use the VPN. Please refer to:

17 Configure WireGuard VPN Clients

Enjoy your very own VPN!

17 Configure WireGuard VPN Clients

WireGuard VPN clients (https://www.wireguard.com/install/) are available for Windows, macOS, iOS and Android.

To add a VPN connection, open the WireGuard App on your mobile device, tap the "Add" button, then scan the generated QR code in the script output.

For Windows and macOS, first securely transfer the generated `.conf` file to your computer, then open WireGuard and import the file.

To manage WireGuard VPN clients, run the install script again: `sudo bash wireguard.sh`. See Chapter 18 for more details.

- Platforms
  - Windows
  - OS X (macOS)
  - Android
  - iOS (iPhone/iPad)

WireGuard VPN clients: https://www.wireguard.com/install/

17.1 Windows

1. Securely transfer the generated `.conf` file to your computer.
2. Install and launch the **WireGuard** VPN client.
3. Click **Import tunnel(s) from file**.
4. Browse to and select the `.conf` file, then click **Open**.
5. Click **Activate**.

17.2 OS X (macOS)

1. Securely transfer the generated `.conf` file to your computer.

2. Install and launch the **WireGuard** App from **App Store**.

3. Click **Import tunnel(s) from file**.

4. Browse to and select the `.conf` file, then click **Open**.

5. Click **Activate**.

17.3 Android

1. Install and launch the **WireGuard** App from **Google Play**.

2. Tap the "+" button, then tap **Scan from QR code**.

3. Scan the generated QR code in the output of the VPN script.

4. Enter anything you like for the **Tunnel Name**.

5. Tap **Create tunnel**.

6. Slide the switch ON for the new VPN profile.

17.4 iOS (iPhone/iPad)

1. Install and launch the **WireGuard** App from **App Store**.

2. Tap **Add a tunnel**, then tap **Create from QR code**.

3. Scan the generated QR code in the output of the VPN script.

4. Enter anything you like for the tunnel name.

5. Tap **Save**.

6. Slide the switch ON for the new VPN profile.

18 WireGuard: Manage VPN Clients

After setting up WireGuard on your server, you can manage WireGuard VPN clients by following the instructions in this chapter. For example, you can add new VPN client(s) on the server for your additional computers and mobile devices, list existing clients, or remove an existing client.

To manage WireGuard VPN clients, first connect to your server using SSH, then run:

```
sudo bash wireguard.sh
```

You will see the following options:

```
WireGuard is already installed.

Select an option:
 1) Add a new client
 2) List existing clients
 3) Remove an existing client
 4) Remove WireGuard
 5) Exit
Option:
```

You can then enter your desired option to add, list or remove WireGuard VPN client(s).

Note: These options may change in newer versions of the script. Read carefully before selecting your desired option.

18.1 Add a new client

To add a new WireGuard VPN client:

1. Select option 1 from the menu, by typing 1 and pressing enter.
2. Provide a name for the new client.

3. Select a DNS server for the new client, which will be used while connected to the VPN.

Next steps: Configure WireGuard VPN clients. See Chapter 17 for more details.

18.2 List existing clients

Select option 2 from the menu, by typing 2 and pressing enter. The script will then display a list of existing WireGuard VPN clients.

18.3 Remove a client

To remove an existing WireGuard VPN client:

1. Select option 3 from the menu, by typing 3 and pressing enter.
2. From the list of existing clients, select the client you want to remove.
3. Confirm the client removal.

About the Author

Lin Song, PhD, is a Software Engineer and open source developer. He created and maintains the Setup IPsec VPN projects on GitHub since 2014, for building your own VPN server in just a few minutes. The projects have 20,000+ GitHub stars and 30 million+ Docker pulls, and have helped millions of users set up their own VPN servers.

Connect with Lin Song
GitHub: https://github.com/hwdsl2
LinkedIn: https://www.linkedin.com/in/linsongui

Thanks for reading! I do hope you get the best from reading this book. If this book was helpful to you, I'd be very grateful if you leave a rating or post a short review.

Thanks,
Lin Song
Author

Made in the USA
Coppell, TX
19 September 2023

21632952R00077